Studies in International Economics

Financing, Adjustment, and the International Monetary Fund

Peter B. Kenen

THE BROOKINGS INSTITUTION
Washington, D.C.

©*1986 by*

THE BROOKINGS INSTITUTION

1775 Massachusetts Avenue, N.W., Washington, D.C. 20036

Library of Congress Catalog Card Number
ISBN 0-8157-4883-3

9 8 7 6 5 4 3 2 1

Financing, Adjustment,
and the
International Monetary Fund

Studies in International Economics

THE BROOKINGS INSTITUTION is an independent organization devoted to nonpartisan research, education, and publication in economics, government, foreign policy, and the social sciences generally. Its principal purposes are to aid in the development of sound public policies and to promote public understanding of issues of national importance.

The Institution was founded on December 8, 1927, to merge the activities of the Institute for Government Research, founded in 1916, the Institute of Economics, founded in 1922, and the Robert Brookings Graduate School of Economics and Government, founded in 1924.

The Board of Trustees is responsible for the general administration of the Institution, while the immediate direction of the policies, program, and staff is vested in the President, assisted by an advisory committee of the officers and staff. The by-laws of the Institution state: "It is the function of the Trustees to make possible the conduct of scientific research, and publication, under the most favorable conditions, and to safeguard the independence of the research staff in the pursuit of their studies and in the publication of the results of such studies. It is not a part of their function to determine, control, or influence the conduct of particular investigations or the conclusions reached."

The President bears final responsibility for the decision to publish a manuscript as a Brookings book. In reaching his judgment on the competence, accuracy, and objectivity of each study, the President is advised by the director of the appropriate research program and weighs the views of a panel of expert outside readers who report to him in confidence on the quality of the work. Publication of a work signifies that it is deemed a competent treatment worthy of public consideration but does not imply endorsement of conclusions or recommendations.

The Institution maintains its position of neutrality on issues of public policy in order to safeguard the intellectual freedom of the staff. Hence interpretations or conclusions in Brookings publications should be understood to be solely those of the authors and should not be attributed to the Institution, to its trustees, officers, or other staff members, or to the organizations that support its research.

Foreword

The international economic crises of the last decade, the oil shocks of 1974–75 and 1979–80, the recession of 1981–82, and the onset of serious debt problems made heavy demands on the resources of the International Monetary Fund. Large increases in Fund quotas helped to meet those demands, but the Fund was also obliged to borrow from some of its members and to make major modifications in the policies governing use of its resources.

In this study Peter B. Kenen examines the evolution of the Fund as a financial institution and argues that the modifications made in the last decade have altered the fundamental character of the institution. He reexamines the rationale for some of the Fund's policies, including repayment requirements and conditionality. These issues are reviewed in a broad analytical framework in which the use of Fund credit is treated as one of several sources of financing available to countries with balance-of-payments problems. Finally, the author proposes reforms of the financial structure of the Fund to give more weight to its role as a reserve-creating institution and to provide for more orderly expansion of its own activities.

Peter B. Kenen is Walker Professor of Economics and International Finance and Director of the International Finance Section at Princeton University. He is indebted to W. Max Corden for many helpful conversations during a visit to the Australian National University on a professorial fellowship award by the Reserve Bank of Australia, and to Arminio Fraga for useful suggestions for dealing with some of the issues in the appendix. He is also grateful for valuable comments by Ralph C. Bryant, Richard N. Cooper, Andrew D. Crockett, Sidney Dell, Manuel Guitian, Rachel McCulloch, Jacques J. Polak, Walter W. Salant, Robert Solomon, John Williamson, Johannes Witteveen, and several participants in a workshop on the evolution of the International Monetary Fund held at Brookings on January 7, 1985. Brenda B. Szittya edited the manuscript, and Carolyn Rutsch verified its factual content.

This study was supported by an experimental grant in international economic policy awarded to the Brookings Institution by the National Science Foundation. The views expressed here are those of the author and should not be ascribed to those who commented on the manuscript, to the National Science Foundation, or to the officers, trustees, or staff members of the Brookings Institution.

BRUCE K. MAC LAURY
President

February 1986
Washington, D.C.

THE International Monetary Fund has been extremely active in the last ten years. In the wake of the 1974–75 and 1979–80 oil shocks, it assisted in "recycling" the balance of payments surpluses of the oil-exporting countries by creating special facilities to finance the deficits of oil-importing countries. With the onset of the international debt crisis in 1982, it made its own financial resources available on an unprecedented scale, and used them catalytically to generate net lending by commercial banks. Without the Fund's endorsement of a debtor country's policies, the banks would not agree to reschedule repayments or make new loans; without the banks' participation, however, the Fund would not make its own resources available. Much has been written about these activities, but the literature has concentrated on the Fund's influence over national policies—the particular commitments that governments must make to qualify for access to the Fund's resources and the changing character of those commitments.[1] Less attention has been paid to the implications of the Fund's activities for its own structure and characteristics as an international financial institution.

This study concentrates on those implications. It examines the role of the Fund as a supplier of balance of payments financing—as a source of reserve credit broadly defined and of reserves narrowly defined. It looks at the ways in which the Fund has obtained resources and in which it has made them available to members. It shows how these financial practices have changed in recent years and suggests that the changes have altered the fundamental nature of the institution in ways that were not foreseen by its founders and that may be damaging to its future. It examines the influence of the Fund on its members' policies, including the policy conditions it attaches to the use of its resources and the more general influence it seeks to exert through the consultations and other procedures by which it tries to exercise "surveillance" over the exchange rate policies of its members. This study is less concerned with the nature of that influence, however, than with the rationale for it and for other characteristics of the Fund's transactions. Must drawings on the Fund be repaid to protect the integrity and liquidity of the Fund itself? Do these same desiderata justify the Fund's insistence on obtaining policy commitments from governments

---

1. See John Williamson, ed., *IMF Conditionality* (Washington, D.C.: Institute for International Economics, 1983), and sources cited there.

that seek to use its resources? To what extent should the Fund concentrate its efforts on the creation of reserves, as contrasted with credit facilities? Can one expect the Fund's own reserve asset, the special drawing right (SDR), to play a larger role in the monetary system and in the activities of the Fund itself?

The study begins by reviewing the evolution of the Fund and raising issues for subsequent discussion. Next, it examines the main considerations that bear on the choice facing a country with a balance of payments deficit—the choice between financing and adjustment—because that is the context in which the Fund's activities must be appraised. Thereafter, it looks closely at considerations that bear on the choice among methods of financing, including the use of reserves and reserve credit and of official borrowing from international financial markets. This discussion leads, in turn, to an examination of the conditions that attach to the use of Fund credit, including repayment terms and policy requirements. Finally, the study reexamines the role and internal structure of the Fund in light of conclusions reached in earlier sections.

The Fund as a Financial Institution

Analogies can be helpful in trying to characterize a complicated institution, as long as they are used judiciously. They are particularly helpful in sorting out ideas about the International Monetary Fund and tracing its evolution as an international financial institution.

Four Prototypes

All financial institutions are intermediaries, in that they mobilize resources by issuing liabilities and use those resources to acquire earning assets. Nevertheless, they differ fundamentally in the nature of their liabilities and, therefore, in the terms on which they can expand their activities.

A community of households can be expected to establish four financial institutions:

—a bank to facilitate transactions between households by providing a convenient means of payment (money);

—a credit union to help households borrow from each other in order to bridge temporary gaps between their payments and receipts;

—an insurance company to provide protection against calamities that occur with predictable frequency but not predictable incidence; and

—an investment trust to bring together households with different needs and opportunities, including entrepreneurial opportunities.

2

All four institutions will accumulate resources and use them to make loans or investments, but each institution's size will be determined by a different set of forces.

Because the bank will be established primarily to provide a means of payment, its size will be determined by the households' demand for that means of payment, which will depend on the volume of transactions among them and on the opportunity costs of holding money.[2] Banks are regulated carefully because they must meet the community's need for an efficient payments system but can exploit that need by making risky loans and investments. Prudential regulation is concerned to prevent bank failures, which can impair the integrity of the payments system. Monetary regulation is concerned to prevent gross discrepancies between the demand for money and the nominal quantity supplied by banks— discrepancies that can be removed only by changing the price level.

The credit union will meet needs arising from short-term and life-cycle differences between households' earnings and outlays. These needs do not represent fundamental differences in households' opportunities; on the contrary, they represent a basic similarity in households' expectations. Because households expect to be borrowers from time to time, they undertake to be lenders at other times and thus enter into reciprocal commitments, which determine the size of the union itself. It can therefore be said that a credit union functions on the principle of mutuality, encompassing its members' expectations and commitments. Members may not have automatic access; they may have to demonstrate their creditworthiness before they can borrow. But the union is expected to treat them uniformly.[3]

---

2. It is sometimes important to distinguish between two types of banks. Some must stand ready to convert their liabilities into other forms of money; this is the case with ordinary commercial banks. Others issue liabilities that are not convertible; this is the case with central banks that are not rigidly committed to a fixed exchange rate or link with gold. Triffin's plan for reform of the IMF would have put it in the first class; the IMF would have been required to sell gold for bancor. See Robert Triffin, *Gold and the Dollar Crisis: The Future of Convertibility* (Yale University Press, 1960), p. 112. Keynes's plan for a clearing union would have put it in the second class and relieved it of the obligation to convert bancor into gold. See Donald Moggridge, ed., *The Collected Writings of John Maynard Keynes*, vol. 25: *Activities 1940–44, Shaping the Post-War World: The Clearing Union* (Macmillan, 1980), p. 184. I will argue below, however, that Keynes's clearing union was less like a bank than Triffin's IMF.

3. The notion of uniformity is enshrined in the practices of the IMF and commonly interpreted to mean that members in similar circumstances should receive similar treatment. On the view taken here, the notion of uniformity derives from the more basic principle of mutuality. Members acquire the right to borrow from a credit union by committing themselves to lend to the union.

An insurance company will be created because households cannot protect themselves from unevenly distributed calamities. If all households were certain to suffer small losses once in a while but were immune to large ones, they would self-insure (and join a credit union to make it easier). When, instead, some households can be expected to suffer large losses, and no one knows which ones or when, all of them will pool their risks by creating an insurance firm. Its size will be determined by the range and characteristics of the calamities against which it offers financial protection and by the intensity of the households' risk aversion.

An investment trust will serve those households having needs or opportunities fundamentally different from those of other households. It will achieve its purpose, however, only by offering better terms than households could obtain by dealing directly with each other. The pooling of risks and maturities is at issue here, but skill in risk assessment is even more important. An investment trust must exercise selectivity in a manner inimical to the principle of mutuality that governs the functioning of a credit union. Its size will therefore depend on the extent of heterogeneity among households, which determines the volume of investment opportunities, and on the efficiency with which it can identify and rank those opportunities.

Classifying the Fund

How should the IMF be classified? Max Corden has compared it to an insurance company, because it protects its members from certain calamities, including self-inflicted ones.[4] But the similarity ends there. Although there is an actuarial relationship between the premiums collected by an insurance company and its total payments to its policyholders, the premiums paid by an individual policyholder do not limit the benefits paid to that policyholder when a calamity strikes. Furthermore, the benefits are not loans; the policyholder does not have to pay them back.

By contrast, most drawings on the Fund must be paid back, and the amount that a member can draw from the Fund is determined by that

4. W. M. Corden, "Is There an Important Role for an International Reserve Asset Such as the SDR?," in George M. von Furstenberg, ed., *International Money and Credit: The Policy Roles* (IMF, 1983), p. 226. Corden's analogy is flawed for reasons mentioned in the text and because it leads him to treat the problem of moral hazard as the basic justification for conditionality. The problem of moral hazard calls for preventive measures rather than corrective measures. It may therefore justify Fund surveillance, broadly defined, but not Fund conditionality.

member's quota, which also determines its subscription to the Fund's resources. Thus, the Fund is much more like a credit union, with relations among its members based on the principle of mutuality.

More precisely, the Fund began as a credit union. Strict mutuality has broken down in recent years, as the Fund has relied increasingly on borrowing from some of its members in order to meet the needs of other members and in recognition of fundamental differences among its members' needs. As a consequence, the scale of its operations has come to depend in part on its ability to borrow. Furthermore, the Fund has engaged in risk reduction by imposing policy conditions on its members, and has acted not only on behalf of its creditors but also on behalf of other intermediaries, including commercial banks.

Some had thought or hoped that the Fund would evolve in a different direction—that it would begin to function as a bank by meeting its members' needs for international money (reserves). That was the expectation on which Robert Triffin based his 1960 plan for reform of the IMF, and it was the basis for recommendations made in my recent paper on ways to expand the use of the SDR.[5] The same expectation surfaced even earlier, in the debates that preceded the establishment of the Fund, and it led some participants to favor John Maynard Keynes's plan for a clearing union rather than Harry Dexter White's plan for a stabilization fund, which became the basis for the Articles of Agreement of the Fund in 1944. But both were plans for a credit union, in which a member's access to balance of payments credit was based on a quota and on a reciprocal commitment to grant credit to others. Neither was a plan for a bank with credit-creating powers dependent on its members' demand for reserves.[6]

The two plans differed mainly in the way that they defined the creditors' commitments. Under Keynes's plan, there was no clear limit to the amount of credit that a surplus country had to grant; in principle, one member, by itself, could have been required to lend an amount equal to all other members' quotas. Under White's plan, each member's obligation was related indirectly to that member's quota, and under the actual Fund agreement, it was limited explicitly by the member's quota. Under that agreement, the Fund was to grant credit on behalf of its members by

5. Triffin, *Gold and the Dollar Crisis,* and Peter B. Kenen, "Use of the SDR to Supplement or Substitute for Other Means of Finance," in von Furstenberg, ed., *International Money and Credit,* pp. 341–58.

6. For an interesting comparison of the two plans that agrees broadly with the comparison in the text see Keynes's own memorandum in Moggridge, ed., *Activities 1940–44,* pp. 215–26.

selling some members' currencies to others, and initial holdings of each member's currency were defined by the member's quota.[7]

The two plans were also similar in that they would have allowed members to draw freely on their quotas, without meeting explicit conditions, and would not have required that drawings be repaid. In this respect, moreover, both plans differed crucially from the arrangements actually adopted at Bretton Woods. Under the original Fund agreement, a country joining the Fund made a subscription equal to its quota, paying one quarter in gold and the remainder in its own currency. The Fund's initial holdings of the member's currency were thus smaller than the member's quota, and this difference defined the member's reserve position. A member was able to draw freely on its reserve position merely by making a representation of balance of payments need. When it went further, however, the Fund had to satisfy itself that the drawing was consistent with the Articles of Agreement and with Fund policies adopted under them. Furthermore, such drawings had to be repaid.

The original arrangements have been modified somewhat. For example, a member now pays a quarter of any quota increase in SDRs or currencies approved by the Fund, rather than in gold. Nevertheless, members use their reserve positions and their access to Fund credit in the same basic way that they did originally. When a member draws on the Fund, it sells its own currency to the Fund in exchange for the currencies of other members or for SDRs. As it does so, the Fund's holdings of its currency rise, and the member's reserve position falls. If the member's drawing is larger than a quarter of its quota, its reserve position goes to zero, and the member is said to be using Fund credit. It may go on doing so, subject to Fund approval, until the Fund's holdings of its currency reach 200 percent of the member's quota (so that its use of Fund credit is equal to its quota). A member's use of Fund credit is measured in quarters of quota, and there are thus four credit tranches available. Normally, the Fund imposes

7. Under the original Articles of Agreement, the remaining quarter of each member's quota was subscribed in gold, which meant that the United States had a larger obligation than any other member to provide credit through the Fund because it was the only member committed to buy gold. (In effect, its obligation was equal to the Fund's total holdings of dollars and gold and thus equal to the whole U.S. quota *plus* one quarter of all other members' quotas.) Under the Second Amendment to the Articles of Agreement, which entered into force in 1978, the fourth quarter of any increase in quotas is to be subscribed in special drawing rights. Had this amendment been in force initially, the members' obligations would have been fully symmetrical, because each member's obligation to accept SDRs, directly from the Fund or from other members, is limited by its quota. (Strictly, its acceptance limit is based on its cumulative allocation of SDRs, but its allocation is based on its quota.)

6

stricter policy conditions as members move into the higher credit tranches.[8]

The Advent of the SDR

In 1969, the Fund Articles of Agreement were amended to authorize the creation of special drawing rights, which would be treated as reserve assets and, therefore, a form of international money. Many saw this amendment as the first in a series of steps that would convert the Fund into a bank; once certain restrictions were relaxed, the Fund would be able to meet its members' needs for balance of payments credit by "printing" its own money. The scale of its operations would be limited only by the demand for reserves, just as those of banks, taken collectively, are limited by the demand for money.

A close look at those restrictions, however, leads one to a different view. The 1969 amendment extended the Fund's role but did not change it fundamentally, because the Fund's ability to provide balance of payments credit was still governed by the principle of mutuality.

A bank creates money in the process of creating credit—by making additional loans and investments. The 1969 amendment authorized the Fund to create and distribute SDRs without comparable credit creation on the part of the Fund itself; the SDRs were to be allocated to each member in proportion to its quota.[9] Once SDRs were issued, moreover, their use was severely circumscribed. Voluntary transfers between members typically required the consent of the Fund, and SDRs could be used for balance of payments financing only within boundaries defined by a reconstitution requirement and an acceptance limit.[10]

8. This brief description needs to be amended in two ways—one technical and one historical. The technical amendment has to do with drawings by other members. If a member of the Fund purchases another member's currency before that other member makes a drawing of its own, the Fund's holdings of the other member's currency will fall, raising the member's reserve position and thus the amount it can draw on reserve position terms. The historical amendment has to do with the widening of access to Fund resources in the 1970s. As a result of that process, described later, a member's access to Fund credit is not necessarily limited to the four credit tranches. The credit tranche policy continues to govern access to resources *owned* by the Fund (those that come from members' subscriptions); the widening of access and policies pertaining to it relate to the use of resources *borrowed* by the Fund. For a detailed account of the Fund's arrangements and practices, see Anand G. Chandarvarkar, *The International Monetary Fund: Its Financial Organization and Activities,* IMF Pamphlet Series 42 (IMF, 1984).

9. In this sense, SDRs are "outside" money, whereas deposits created by bank lending are "inside" money.

10. Transfers could be made without the Fund's consent only when a member agreed to use SDRs when redeeming another member's holdings of its currency.

7

Under the reconstitution requirement, each SDR holder was expected to maintain an average SDR balance over any five-year period no smaller than 30 percent of its average cumulative SDR allocation. It could use all its SDRs some of the time and some of them all the time, but it could not use all of them all the time. Under the acceptance limit, a member was not required to accept SDRs from other members or from the Fund itself if its holdings had already reached 300 percent of its cumulative allocation.

When it was introduced, the SDR was often described as paper gold because of the basic reason for creating it—to impart elasticity to the supply of reserves and thus "meet the need, as and when it arises, for a supplement to existing reserve assets" (Article XV, sec. 1). But the nickname was appropriate for a different reason. Under the 1969 rules, an SDR allocation resembled an increase in reserve positions, which was obtainable at that time only by making a gold payment to the Fund when subscribing to an increase in Fund quotas. There were (and are still) differences in the interest costs of using SDRs and drawing on reserve positions, and the reconstitution requirement was less onerous than the full-repayment rule that applied at that time to drawings on reserve positions. Nevertheless, the rights and opportunities conferred by an SDR allocation were more like those conferred by an increase in reserve positions than those conferred by holding gold outright. The SDR was paper gold not because its attributes resembled those of gold or other reserve assets held outside the Fund but because an SDR allocation gave members an asset much like a reserve position in the Fund without requiring them to part with gold.

The original restrictions on transfers have been relaxed. One member can now transfer SDRs to another without the Fund's consent. If no other member will take them voluntarily, the Fund will designate a recipient. For this purpose, however, the member seeking to make the transfer must make a representation of balance of payments need, and the Fund cannot force a designee to take SDRs in excess of the designee's acceptance limit.[11] In 1981, moreover, the reconstitution requirement was dropped,

11. Designation was part of the 1969 package and is tied up closely with the acceptance limit. It underwrites the transferability of the SDR, protecting the interests of members that expect to use their holdings. The acceptance limit spreads the burden of maintaining transferability, protecting the interests of members that can expect to be designated. I have argued elsewhere that both rules should be allowed to atrophy. Eventually, the transferability of the SDR should be guaranteed by increasing its usefulness, which means, in turn, making it transferable between official and private institutions. (See Kenen, "Use of the SDR," pp. 342–43.) Until that is done, however, designation will be needed, and it may thus be impossible to eliminate the acceptance limit. It should be noted, moreover, that the size of the acceptance limit is written into the Fund agreement, in Article XIX, sec. 4(a), and can be changed only by amending it.

making the SDR more like a reserve asset held outside the Fund (but without diminishing its resemblance to a reserve position in the Fund, because the full-repayment rule no longer applies to drawings on reserve positions). Yet there have been no changes in two other practices. SDR allocations must be made in proportion to quotas, and the acceptance limit remains in place, and these practices work together to preserve the principle of mutuality. They limit the amount of balance of payments credit that each member has to extend through the Fund.

The Origins of Borrowing

The nature of the Fund did not begin to change until the 1970s, when it started to finance its activities by borrowing. The scale of its operations ceased to depend exclusively on subscriptions made by members in order to obtain drawing rights of their own. It started to depend in part on the Fund's ability to borrow from one group of members in order to meet the needs of others. In effect, the Fund became less like a credit union based on the principle of mutuality and more like a simple financial intermediary—an institution of the sort represented earlier by a prototypical investment trust.[12]

Strictly speaking, the transformation began in 1963, with the creation of the compensatory financing facility (CFF). The CFF represented a departure from the principle of mutuality, because it was meant to meet the special needs of a subset of Fund members—developing countries heavily dependent on exports of primary products. The breach of principle was modest, however, as was the size of the CFF itself, and it served to uphold another principle: countries experiencing shortfalls in their export earnings should seek financial assistance rather than adopt price-stabilizing schemes that distort trade flows and resource allocation. Furthermore, creation of the CFF did not involve borrowing by the Fund, and that was the step that started to blur the Fund's identity.

The Fund's right to borrow was established from the start, but only to permit it to discharge its existing obligations, not to enlarge its operations. Under the quota-based rules that govern subscriptions and drawings, the Fund's liquidity will be impaired if many members with large quotas seek simultaneously or in quick succession to draw all they can from the Fund. It will not be able to satisfy their claims. As a practical matter, moreover,

12. Although a credit union *is* an intermediary, that term is used hereafter as it is in this paragraph—to describe an institution whose size depends on its ability to borrow from one group of households, firms, or countries in order to lend to others, as distinct from one whose size depends on its members' prior commitments.

the Fund's liquidity can be impaired by a few large drawings, because many currencies held by the Fund are hard to use for balance of payments financing. The United States, for example, would want German marks or Japanese yen for exchange market intervention, not Mexican pesos or Saudi riyals.

The liquidity problem was anticipated in the Fund agreement, although the agreement focused on a different possibility, that one member of the Fund would run a large balance of payments surplus, making its currency "scarce" in general and depleting the Fund's holdings of that currency. Under Article VII, sec. 1, of the Fund agreement, the so-called Scarce Currency Clause, the Fund is authorized to

> propose to the member that, on terms and conditions agreed between the Fund and the member, the latter lend its currency to the Fund or that, with the concurrence of the member, the Fund borrow such currency from some other source either within or outside the territories of the member, but no member shall be under any obligation to make such loans to the Fund or to concur in the borrowing of its currency by the Fund from any other source.[13]

The General Arrangements to Borrow (GAB), which came into effect in 1962, were based on Article VII and were designed explicitly to protect the Fund's liquidity. Ten industrial countries agreed in advance to lend their currencies to the Fund "when supplementary resources are needed to forestall or cope with an impairment of the international monetary system" but only when one of the participants was about to make a drawing on the Fund.[14] Like the CFF, the GAB was meant to meet the needs of a subset of Fund members. Unlike the CFF, it did not derogate from mutuality. The ten participants took on obligations to each other in order to protect their own access to Fund credit. The principle was breached in 1983, however, when the Fund was empowered to invoke the GAB and make calls on the participants in order to finance drawings by nonparticipants. At that point, the GAB became part of the broader credit network

---

13. Article VII, sec. 1(i). This language has forced the Fund into some fancy footwork. When it borrowed from Saudi Arabia in order to finance the widening of access to Fund credit, it had to borrow Saudi riyals. Therefore, its agreement with Saudi Arabia had to provide that Saudi Arabia would buy them back with a freely usable currency.

14. For the full text, see International Monetary Fund, *Annual Report of the Executive Board for the Financial Year Ended April 30, 1962*, pp. 234–45. Hereafter IMF, *Annual Report, 19–*. Switzerland adhered to the GAB in 1964. Ironically, the Scarce Currency Clause was designed to anticipate a dollar shortage (the need for other members to draw dollars from the Fund), but the GAB was put in place to deal with a dollar glut (the need by the United States to draw on the Fund).

built up by the Fund in the 1970s, though it remains distinct, in that it can be invoked only for the purpose of defending the stability of the monetary system as a whole.[15]

The Advent of Intermediation

The first use of borrowing to enlarge the Fund's operations—to provide Fund credit in amounts larger than those defined by the quota-based credit tranches—took place immediately after the first oil shock. The Fund borrowed SDR 3.0 billion from nine countries to establish the first oil facility in 1974, and it borrowed another SDR 3.8 billion from fourteen countries to establish a second in 1975. A member was permitted to draw on these facilities, subject to certain limitations relating to the increase in its oil bill, reserves, and Fund quota, if the Fund was satisfied that "the member needs assistance because of increases in the cost of its imports of petroleum . . . and because it has a balance of payments need."[16] The member was not forced to make a simultaneous credit tranche drawing that would subject it to conditionality, but loose conditions were attached to drawings on the second oil facility.[17]

A total of fifty-five members used the two oil facilities, purchasing the equivalent of SDR 6.9 billion. Purchases amounting to 37 percent of the total were made by forty-five developing countries, including India, Korea, Chile, and Pakistan. Purchases by two industrial countries, Italy and the United Kingdom, accounted for 35 percent, and eight other developed countries accounted for the remaining 28 percent.[18] By mid-1983, however, all drawings on the two facilities had been repaid, and the Fund

---

15. For the revised text, see IMF, *Annual Report, 1983*, pp. 146–53, especially par. 21, under which the managing director may initiate a call on the GAB in connection with drawings by nonparticipants "if, after consultation, he considers that the Fund faces an inadequacy of resources to meet actual and expected requests for financing that reflect the existence of an exceptional situation associated with balance of payments problems of members of a character or aggregate size that could threaten the stability of the international monetary system." This language can be reconciled with the principle of mutuality. The participants can be said to be purchasing insurance against threats to the stability of the monetary system that would do more harm to them than to the nonparticipants whose drawings would be financed by the GAB. But this interpretation of mutuality is somewhat looser than the one embodied in the earlier version of the GAB.

16. IMF, *Annual Report, 1974*, p. 122.

17. IMF, *Annual Report, 1975*, p. 94, and A. W. Hooke, *The International Monetary Fund: Its Evolution, Organization, and Activities*, IMF Pamphlet Series 37, 3d ed. (IMF, 1983), pp. 56–57.

18. IMF, *Annual Report, 1976*, p. 54.

itself had repaid the original lenders. The first exercise in intermediation had been fully liquidated.[19]

In 1977, however, two full years before the second oil shock, the Interim Committee launched another exercise in intermediation:

> Given the persistence of large payments imbalances, important demands for the Fund's resources can be expected to materialize. The Committee found good grounds for believing that expansion of the Fund's role as a *financial intermediary* could contribute significantly to promotion of international adjustment and to maintenance of confidence in the continued expansion of the world economy. . . .
>
> The Committee recognized that there was an urgent need for a supplementary arrangement of a *temporary* nature that would enable the Fund to expand its financial assistance to those of its members that in the next several years will face payments imbalances that are large in relation to their economies.
>
> The Committee agreed that some of the main features of this supplementary arrangement would be as follows:
>
> (i) The Fund would establish substantial lines of credit in order to be able to assist members to meet their needs for supplementary assistance.
>
> (ii) Access to assistance under the supplementary arrangement should be available to all members and should be subject to adequate conditionality, and such assistance should normally be provided on the basis of a standby arrangement covering a period longer than one year. . . .[20]

The supplementary financing facility (SFF) came into being early in 1979, after the Fund had arranged to borrow SDR 7.8 billion from fourteen countries (including SDR 1.9 billion from Saudi Arabia, SDR 1.5 billion from the United States, and SDR 1.1 billion from Germany). To meet the requirement laid down by the Interim Committee that assistance from the SFF should be subject to adequate conditionality, drawings on the SFF were tied directly to credit tranche drawings. A member drawing on its first credit tranche could draw an extra 12.5 percent of quota from the SFF; if it went beyond, it could draw an extra 30 percent of quota from the SFF along with each remaining credit tranche. Thus, a member that used all four credit tranches could draw an extra 102.5 percent of quota

---

19. In September 1974, just after establishing the first oil facility, the Fund established the extended Fund facility (EFF), designed to give members financial support for periods longer than those in which credit tranche drawings are normally repaid. Like the CFF before it, the EFF was designed to help a subset of Fund members—those that cannot deal with their balance of payments problems without making major changes in policies and economic structure.

20. Press Communiqué, April 29, 1977, in IMF, *Annual Report, 1977*, p. 115 (emphasis added).

from the SFF, making its total access to Fund credit slightly more than twice as large as its ordinary access.[21]

The SFF was meant to be temporary and was due to expire in 1982, but its resources were fully committed in early 1981. As the need for large drawings was expected to continue in the wake of the second oil shock, the Fund embarked on a third exercise in intermediation, known as the enlarged access policy (EAP). It became operational in mid-1981 and was to last until the next increase in Fund quotas, which was expected to take place in 1984 but was in fact completed in 1983.

The new policy was financed by medium-term borrowing from Saudi Arabia and short-term borrowing from eighteen other countries. It widened access to Fund credit by much more than the SFF. Under the EAP, access to conditional Fund credit (credit tranche and EAP resources) was raised to 150 percent of quota per year or 450 percent of quota for a three-year period. Members were to draw on EAP resources in tandem with regular credit tranche drawings, just as they did under the SFF, but they could go on drawing on those resources after they had reached the old SFF limit.[22]

The Magnitude of Intermediation

Before bringing this story up to date, let us look at table 1, which shows the extent to which Fund credit has been based on borrowing, beginning with the first year of the oil facilities.

In 1975–76, the main years of use of the oil facilities, drawings on borrowed resources totaled SDR 6.5 billion and averaged about SDR 3.2 billion per year. They were very large compared with total drawings, reaching 60.2 percent in 1976, and were even higher compared with total conditional drawings, reaching 89.4 percent, because members could

---

21. Slightly different rules were applied to SFF drawings connected with EFF drawings rather than regular credit tranche drawings, and this was also the case with the EAP, discussed below. All drawings on the SFF were made by developing countries, whereas industrial countries had drawn heavily on the oil facilities.

22. The 450 percent limit was supplemented by a 600 percent cumulative limit on the use of Fund resources (excluding use of the oil, compensatory financing, and buffer stock facilities). The limit was meant to prevent members from drawing on EAP resources if they had already drawn heavily on credit tranche, EFF, and SFF resources. When the EAP limits were reduced in 1984 and 1985, this cumulative limit was reduced proportionately. There was also a small modification in the rules linking credit tranche drawings with the use of EAP resources. As in the case of the SFF, members drawing on the EFF were subject to slightly different rules than members drawing on the credit tranches.

Table 1. *Drawings on Fund Facilities, 1975–84, Years Ending April 30*
SDR millions

Year	Total	Reserve tranche	Compensatory financing facility[a]	Conditional Total	Conditional Ordinary resources[b]	Conditional Borrowed resources[c]	Borrowed resources as a percentage of Total	Borrowed resources as a percentage of Conditional
1975	5,103	982	18	4,103	1,604	2,499	49.0	60.9
1976	6,591	1,324	832	4,435	469	3,966	60.2	89.4
1977	4,910	161	1,753	2,997	2,560	437	8.9	14.6
1978	2,503	136	322	2,045	2,045	0	0	0
1979	3,720	2,480	512	727	727	0	0	0
1980	2,433	223	889	1,321	819	502	20.6	38.0
1981	4,860	474	784	3,602	2,086	1,516	31.2	42.1
1982	8,041	1,080	1,635	5,326	2,110	3,216	40.0	60.4
1983	11,392	1,134	4,092	6,165	3,025	3,141	27.6	50.9
1984	11,518	1,354	1,282	8,882	3,763	5,119	44.4	57.6
Total	61,071	9,348	12,119	39,604	19,208	20,396	33.4	51.5

Source: International Monetary Fund, *Annual Reports*, various years. Detail may not add to total because of rounding.
a. Includes small drawings on the buffer stock facility.
b. Includes drawings on both the credit tranches and the extended Fund facility; also includes drawings financed by calls on the General Arrangements to Borrow (GAB).
c. Includes drawings on oil facilities and supplementary financing facility and borrowings to finance enlarged access policy.

draw on the oil facilities without drawing simultaneously on ordinary sources of Fund credit; they could substitute use of the oil facilities for use of the credit tranches.[23]

In 1980–81, the main years of the SFF, drawings on borrowed resources totaled SDR 2.0 billion and averaged about SDR 1.0 billion per year. In those two years, then, drawings on borrowed resources were much smaller compared with total drawings than they had been in 1975–76, reaching only 31.2 percent in 1981, and were likewise smaller compared with total conditional drawings, because members could not draw on the SFF without also drawing on the credit tranches.

In 1982–84, the years of the EAP, drawings on borrowed resources totaled SDR 11.5 billion and averaged about SDR 3.8 billion per year. They were almost four times as large as average annual drawings under the SFF and were distinctly larger compared with total conditional drawings, because the EAP rules were more liberal than the SFF rules. But they were not much larger compared with total drawings, because reserve tranche and CFF drawings were very high during those same years.

For the ten-year period as a whole, borrowed resources totaled SDR 20.4 billion and averaged about SDR 2.0 billion per year. They accounted for a third of total drawings on the Fund and for slightly more than half of total conditional drawings. These figures support the assertion made before, that the 1970s saw an important change in the character of the Fund.

Second Thoughts

The three exercises in intermediation described above, especially the first and third, were fostered and facilitated by the oil shocks of 1974–75 and 1979–80. Fostered, because the large current account surpluses of the OPEC countries were mirrored by the large current account deficits of other countries, notably those of developing countries, and these latter had to be financed. Facilitated, because the OPEC countries were piling up claims on the rest of the world and were willing, for financial and political

---

23. Drawings on the oil facilities are treated here as conditional drawings, although conditionality was negligible in respect of the first facility and minimal in respect of the second. Drawings financed by calls on the GAB are classified here as drawings on ordinary resources rather than borrowed resources. This is how they are treated in the Fund's tabulations, and the treatment is sensible in light of the distinction stressed above between borrowings designed to replenish liquidity and those designed to increase the scale of activity.

reasons, to lend to the Fund. In other words, "recycling" was required, and the Fund undertook to participate.[24]

In 1982, however, OPEC surpluses shrank sharply, and they disappeared completely in 1983. This shift did not reduce the demand for Fund credit; the need for recycling was replaced by the more urgent need to deal with debt crises—to substitute Fund credit for bank credit in the short term and encourage the resumption of bank lending in the long term. With the disappearance of the OPEC surplus, however, the Fund's ability to borrow was called into question. Who could replace Saudi Arabia as the main supplier of EAP resources? There was talk about Fund borrowing from private markets, but it was opposed by the governments whose currencies the Fund would have to borrow. Therefore, the Fund took steps to limit its borrowing without also curbing access to Fund credit.

Early in 1982, the Fund adopted guidelines to hold down its borrowing. Loans and unused lines of credit should not normally exceed 50 percent of Fund quotas, and they should not exceed 60 percent even in exceptional circumstances.[25]

Early in 1984, after the 1983 increase in Fund quotas, the executive board revised the EAP rules. Access to Fund credit under the EAP was subjected to annual limits ranging from 102 to 125 percent of quota, so that the cumulative three-year limits were cut back from 450 percent of quota to a lower bound of 306 percent and an upper bound of 375 percent. The board pointed out, moreover, that these limits would be ceilings, not targets, and that their application to particular cases would depend on the "seriousness of the member's balance of payments needs and the strength of its adjustment efforts."[26]

As the 1983 increase in Fund quotas averaged 47.5 percent, a strict application of the lower limit (102 percent per year) would freeze the typical member's access to Fund credit. It would stay at 150 percent of the member's old quota. (Use of the upper limit, 125 percent per year, would raise its access to 184 percent of its old quota.) Thus, the 1984 decision

24. In 1974–75, the case for Fund participation was based in part on doubts about the ability of private institutions to do the whole task; there were no precedents. In 1979–81, the case was different. The banks had done well in 1974–75 and continued to lend huge sums thereafter, but there was widespread concern about their ability to do it again. The OPEC surplus was expected to last longer than it did after the first oil shock, and banks had already piled up large claims on developing countries.

25. IMF, *Annual Report, 1982*, p. 125. These are fairly stringent limits, because they make a large allowance for borrowings under the GAB (borrowings actually outstanding or one-half of total credit lines, whichever is bigger).

26. IMF, *Annual Report, 1984*, p. 134. Additional reductions were made in September 1984 and October 1985, bringing the annual limits down to 90 or 110 percent and the three-year limits down to 270 or 330 percent.

altered ex post the role of the increase in Fund quotas. In the past, increases in quotas had raised the Fund's resources but had also raised its members' access to them. Indeed, the increase in access had been the objective, and the increase in resources, the means of achieving it. This time, the quota increase served mainly to raise the Fund's resources and thus to reduce its dependence on borrowing. An increase in access was contemplated in special cases, when the Fund would apply the 125 percent ceiling, but not across the board.

The Fund as a Source of Financing

How has the evolution of the Fund as a financial institution affected its members, viewed as potential clients of the Fund? Where do they stand today, compared with their positions in the early 1970s, before the beginnings of large-scale intermediation?

Table 2 supplies an answer by focusing on the situations of four countries that have been large users of Fund credit. The calculations in that table are hypothetical; to show clearly the effects of changes in Fund policies, each year's calculation assumes that the countries have made no previous drawings on the Fund and that their SDR holdings are intact. It omits the possibility of drawings on the EFF and CFF, which are not available to all members, but allows for the use of Fund-related reserve assets—the member's reserve tranche and its SDR holdings.[27]

The figures for 1973 represent the situation before the first exercise in intermediation. If Argentina's drawing rights and SDR holdings had been intact, that country would have been able to use SDR 262.5 million of Fund-related reserve assets and had access to SDR 440.0 million of Fund credit. Therefore, Fund-related financing could have reached SDR 702.5 million, an amount equal to 40 percent of Argentina's imports.

The figures for 1975 reflect the opening of the oil facilities. As Argentina drew SDR 76.1 million from those facilities, that number is used to represent its access to borrowed resources.[28] Although those facilities made additional financing available through the Fund, the supply of financing fell to 25.8 percent of Argentine imports, because imports rose

27. To avoid double counting, each country's holdings of SDRs are measured by its cumulative allocation less its additional subscriptions in SDRs (or other reserve assets) connected with increases in Fund quotas. Thus, the quota increases of 1978 and 1983 do not affect the countries' holdings of Fund-related reserve assets shown in table 2; their effects on reserve tranches are offset by their effects on SDR holdings.

28. Actual drawings are used instead of potential drawings because access to the oil facilities was based on complex computations that are hard to replicate; see Hooke, *International Monetary Fund*, pp. 56–57.

Table 2. *Calculated Effects of Fund Credit Policies, Quota Changes, and SDR Allocations on Financing Available to Four Countries, 1973–84*

SDR millions

Country and item	1973	1975	1978	1981	1982	1984
Argentina						
Fund-related reserve assets[a]	262.5	262.5	262.5	428.4	428.4	428.4
Credit tranches (= quota)	440.0	440.0	535.0	802.5	802.5	1,113.0
Access to borrowed resources[b]	0.0	76.1	0.0	822.6	2,808.8	2,292.8
Total available through IMF	702.5	778.6	797.5	2,053.5	4,039.7	3,834.2
Total as percentage of prior year's imports	40.0	25.8	22.4	25.4	50.5	91.0[c]
India						
Fund-related reserve assets[a]	597.2	597.2	597.2	916.2	916.2	916.2
Credit tranches (= quota)	940.0	940.0	1,145.0	1,717.5	1,717.5	2,207.7
Access to borrowed resources[b]	0.0	401.3	0.0	1,760.4	6,011.3	4,547.9
Total available through IMF	1,537.2	1,938.5	1,742.2	4,394.1	8,645.0	7,671.8
Total as percentage of prior year's imports	75.1	45.4	30.6	38.5	66.1	60.2
Italy						
Fund-related reserve assets[a]	568.0	568.0	568.0	952.4	952.4	952.4
Credit tranches (= quota)	1,000.0	1,000.0	1,240.0	1,860.0	1,860.0	2,909.1
Access to borrowed resources[b]	0.0	1,455.2	0.0	1,906.5	6,510.0	5,992.7
Total available through IMF	1,568.0	3,023.2	1,808.0	4,718.9	9,322.4	9,854.2
Total as percentage of prior year's imports	8.8	8.8	4.4	6.2	12.1	13.1
United Kingdom						
Fund-related reserve assets[a]	1,706.3	1,706.3	1,706.3	2,613.1	2,613.1	2,613.1
Credit tranches (= quota)	2,800.0	2,800.0	2,925.0	4,387.5	4,387.5	6,194.0
Access to borrowed resources[b]	0.0	1,000.0	0.0	4,497.2	15,356.3	12,759.6
Total available through IMF	4,506.3	5,506.3	4,631.3	11,497.8	22,356.9	21,566.7
Total as percentage of prior year's imports	17.7	12.2	8.6	12.9	25.7	23.0

Source: International Monetary Fund, *International Financial Statistics*, various issues.

a. Figures for reserve assets represent the sum of the country's IMF reserve tranche and cumulative SDR allocation *less* additional subscriptions in SDRs or other reserve assets required by increases in Fund quotas. (As there were no SDR allocations in 1973–78 and 1982–84, increases in Fund quotas that took place in those years did not increase Fund-related reserve assets; their effects were offset by additional subscriptions.)

b. Figures for access to borrowed resources are defined as follows: for 1975, total of actual drawings on oil facilities; for 1981, potential drawings on supplementary financing facility (102.5 percent of quota); for 1982 and 1984, potential drawings on borrowed resources under the enlarged access policy (350 percent of quota for 1982 and 206 percent of quota for 1984). When the credit tranche and EAP figures are added, they yield the three-year access limits (450 percent of quota for 1982 and 306 percent of quota for 1984).

c. Reflects in part a sharp reduction in imports.

faster than financing. (The same thing happened to India and the United Kingdom, but not to Italy, because that country was the largest single user of the oil facilities.)

The figures for 1978 represent the situation after the oil facilities were fully committed but before the next exercise in intermediation. They also show the effects of the quota increase that took place in that year. That quota increase was large enough to raise the supply of financing available to Argentina, but not to the other three countries. In all four cases, moreover, the supply of financing fell compared with imports.

The second exercise in intermediation, involving the SFF, began in 1979 and is represented by the figures for 1981, which include the effects of the quota increase in 1980 and the three-year allocation of SDRs completed in 1981. In all four cases, the supply of financing rose as a percentage of imports but not by enough to restore it to its 1973 level.

The EAP was adopted in 1981 and is represented by the figures for 1982. There was, of course, a very large increase in access to borrowed resources, which rose from 102.5 percent of quota under the SFF to 350 percent of quota under the EAP. And there was as a result a significant increase in the supply of financing relative to imports. (In the Indian case, however, it remained below its 1973 level.)

Finally, the figures for 1984 reflect the situation after the most recent quota increase and the resulting revision of the EAP. They are based on the lower of the two new EAP limits (306 percent of quota), which was meant to keep access constant for the typical Fund member. For three of the four countries shown here, however, the supply of financing fell, because their quotas rose by less than the average for all countries, and it fell in relation to imports for two countries. (It rose compared with imports in the Argentine case because of a sharp drop in imports, and rose in the Italian case because that country's quota rose by more than average.)

Summing up, the supply of financing failed to keep pace with imports until the introduction of the EAP. Under the present version of the EAP, however, supplies of Fund-related financing are not much larger in relation to imports than they were in 1973, before the Fund began to use borrowed resources. (The Indian case, in which the supply of financing fell, is not exceptional; if Argentina's imports had gone on growing, it would have been in the same situation.)

Looking Ahead

When the Fund functioned as a credit union, each member's rights were clearly defined and matched by its obligations. In fact, those obligations

19

were discharged in advance by subscriptions to the Fund's currency pool. It was, of course, impossible for all members to exercise their rights simultaneously, because of limitations on the Fund's liquidity. But the practical effect of that qualification did not greatly impair the balancing of rights and obligations. All members did not need to draw at once, and the limitation on liquidity was relaxed substantially by the GAB.

When the Fund began to rely on borrowing in order to provide additional financing, it altered the balance between rights and obligations. Each member's rights were known, given the Fund's policies regarding the use of borrowed resources, but no member had a clear-cut obligation to provide those resources. The situation was not too murky at first. The Fund did not open its first oil facility (and it limited access to the second) until it had arranged the necessary borrowing. In recent years, however, the Fund has operated under greater uncertainty. It has not known in advance how much it would have to borrow to implement its credit policies, and its ability to borrow large amounts has been called into question by the disappearance of the OPEC surplus.

Borrowing made good sense when OPEC surpluses were large. Indeed, the world might be better off today if the Fund had played a bigger role in the recycling of the surplus—if the oil facilities had been larger and if similar facilities, limited in purpose and fixed in size, had been put in place after the second oil shock.[29] Borrowing makes less sense, however, when current account surpluses are diffused among a variety of countries and the need for balance of payments financing arises mainly from the cutback in bank lending.

It was these concerns, expressed by many members of the Fund, that prompted the three steps taken in 1983–84: the enlargement and revision of the GAB, the quickening of action on the quota increase in 1983, and the downward revision of the EAP limits. These steps represented a shift away from simple intermediation, back to the notion of a quota-based Fund. It must be remembered, however, that the Fund began to borrow because quotas had grown too slowly to meet the need for balance of payments financing. And it is not clear in principle that a quota-based Fund can supply the right sorts of financing.

Let us look at the record. In 1951–55, Fund quotas averaged 10.5 percent of world imports. By 1958, however, they had fallen to 8.7 percent because of the growth of world trade. The first quota increase, in 1959, raised them to 12.5 percent, but they fell again to 8.9 percent in

29. For a different view, see Jacques J. Polak, "The Role of the Fund," in *The International Monetary System: Forty Years After Bretton Woods* (Boston: Federal Reserve Bank of Boston, 1984), pp. 249–51.

1965. At that point, moreover, a pattern set in. Quotas were raised on five occasions, but the first three revisions left them smaller or no larger, relative to imports, than they had been after the previous revision, and the next two revisions did not make up the lost ground. Quotas were raised to 10.5 percent of world imports in 1966 but were down to 9.2 percent by 1968; they were raised to 9.4 percent in 1970 but were down to 3.2 percent by 1977; and they were raised to 3.9 percent in 1978 but fell back to 3.3 percent in 1979. In 1980, quotas were raised to 4.1 percent of world imports, reversing the trend, and to 5.3 percent in 1983. Even after the most recent increase, however, they were less than half as large, relative to imports, as they had been in 1959, after the first increase in Fund quotas.

No one knows the "right" level of Fund quotas; even if it could be ascertained, it would not bear any simple relationship to world imports. But the record is disturbing. If it made sense to raise quotas in 1959 and 1966, when they were much higher relative to imports than after the large increase in 1983, one must question the adequacy of the present quota-raising process—whether it can keep pace with the need for Fund credit.

The larger conceptual issue, whether a quota-based Fund can supply the right sorts of financing, must be studied in the context of considerations bearing on the choice between financing and adjustment and on the choice among methods of financing.

Financing and Adjustment

Much of the literature on financing and adjustment goes back to the years when exchange rates were pegged. The most rigorous contributions came from models that tried to define the optimal stock of reserves—the amount of financing that should be set aside ex ante to deal with balance of payments problems.[30] The literature has not been recast systematically to deal with today's world, in which exchange rates are much more flexible—

30. See, for example, Heinz Robert Heller, "Optimal International Reserves," *Economic Journal*, vol. 76 (June 1966), pp. 296–311; Peter B. Clark, "Demand for International Reserves: A Cross-Country Analysis," *Canadian Journal of Economics*, vol. 3 (November 1970), pp. 577–94; Michael G. Kelly, "The Demand for International Reserves," *American Economic Review*, vol. 60 (September 1970), pp. 655–67; and F. Steb Hipple, *The Disturbance Approach to the Demand for International Reserves*, Princeton Studies in International Finance 35 (Princeton University, International Finance Section, 1974). For critical surveys, see Benjamin J. Cohen, "International Reserves and Liquidity," in Peter B. Kenen, ed., *International Trade and Finance: Frontiers for Research* (Cambridge University Press, 1975), pp. 411–51; and Stanley W. Black, "International Money and International Monetary Arrangements," in Ronald W. Jones and Peter B. Kenen, eds., *Handbook of International Economics*, vol. 2 (Amsterdam: North-Holland, 1985), pp. 1153–93.

even those that do not float. Nor has it been recast to deal systematically with alternative methods of financing. It is dated by its concentration on the use of reserves, a process superseded in the 1970s by the widespread use of borrowing from banks and other private institutions.[31] Finally, the analysis is too static. Some models deal with one dynamic issue, the trade-off between the optimal level of reserves and the speed of balance of payments adjustment.[32] But little is said about the other intertemporal issues that have come to the fore recently in balance of payments theory.[33]

This is not the place to update basic theory. It is appropriate, however, to review the reasons for financing rather than adjusting immediately to balance of payments disturbances and to take account of recent developments in international monetary theory. There has been much new work on optimal modes of adjustment to various shocks[34] and on models in which the evolution of the current account balance reflects intertemporal optimization—in which households borrow or lend on international capital markets to optimize consumption over time and firms borrow or lend to optimize investment—so that balance of payments financing becomes endogenous.[35] One such model is presented in the appendix to this paper and is used to illustrate some assertions in the text (but is far too simple to illustrate others).

31. Corden has taken account of this shift but in a somewhat special model; see W. M. Corden, "The Logic of the International Monetary Non-system," in Fritz Machlup, Gerhard Fels, and Hubertus Müller-Groeling, eds., *Reflections on a Troubled World Economy: Essays in Honor of Herbert Giersch* (St. Martin's Press, 1983), pp. 59–74.

32. See, for example, Jacob A. Frenkel, "International Liquidity and Monetary Control," in von Furstenberg, ed., *International Money and Credit*, pp. 81–85, and sources cited there.

33. For an early reference to those issues, see John Williamson, "Payments Objectives and Economic Welfare," *International Monetary Fund Staff Papers*, vol. 20 (November 1973), p. 587n.

34. See, for example, Jacob A. Frenkel and Joshua Aizenman, "Aspects of the Optimal Management of Exchange Rates," *Journal of International Economics*, vol. 13 (November 1982), pp. 231–56, and Don E. Roper and Stephen J. Turnovsky, "Optimal Exchange Market Intervention in a Simple Stochastic Macro Model," *Canadian Journal of Economics*, vol. 13 (May 1980), pp. 296–309. Both papers deal with stabilization of the domestic economy but reach very different conclusions. Frenkel and Aizenman argue that large real shocks call for pegged exchange rates and large monetary shocks call for floating rates. Roper and Turnovsky reach the more familiar conclusion, based on earlier work by Robert Mundell, that large real shocks call for floating rates and large monetary shocks call for pegged rates. (The two papers differ primarily because Frenkel and Aizenman are concerned with the stabilization of real consumption rather than output or employment, but also because they do not allow monetary shocks to leak out of the economy under pegged exchange rates and do not allow changes in the nominal exchange rate to influence the real rate.) The model in the appendix to this paper belongs to the same family as the Roper-Turnovsky model.

35. See, for example, Jeffrey D. Sachs, "The Current Account and Macroeconomic

Some Definitions

In most of the older literature, decisions concerning financing and adjustment were taken by governments. A government engaged in financing when it used reserves or drew down reserve-credit lines in order to intervene on foreign exchange markets—in order to keep its exchange rate from changing or to limit the change in the rate when it was not pegged. A government engaged in adjustment when it modified its macroeconomic policies to alter the level of aggregate demand or changed its nominal exchange rate in order to change the real exchange rate and thus alter the destination of aggregate demand.

The definition of financing was sometimes extended to cover borrowing by governments and quasi-governmental institutions, although there were debates about borderline cases.[36] The definition was even extended to cover capital flows between private institutions, an extension which implicitly identified adjustment with the elimination of current account deficits and surpluses. But private capital flows were more commonly viewed as forms of adjustment, so that adjustment was implicitly identified with an economy's total response to policies aimed at ending a balance of payments deficit or surplus defined on an official-settlements basis, as well as the economy's endogenous responses to automatic money supply changes of the gold-standard sort and to income changes stemming from current account shocks.[37]

In what follows, financing and adjustment will be defined quite clearly

---

Adjustment in the 1970s," *Brookings Papers on Economic Activity, 1:1981,* pp. 201–68, and *Theoretical Issues in International Borrowing,* Princeton Studies in International Finance 54 (Princeton University, International Finance Section, 1984); Elhanan Helpman, "Inflation and Balance of Payments Adjustments with Maximizing Consumers," in M June Flanders and Assaf Razin, eds., *Development in an Inflationary World* (Academic Press, 1981), pp. 243–58; Maurice Obstfeld, "Capital Mobility and Devaluation in an Optimizing Model with Rational Expectations," *American Economic Review,* vol. 71 (May 1981, *Papers and Proceedings, 1980*), pp. 217–21, and "Macroeconomic Policy, Exchange-Rate Dynamics, and Optimal Asset Accumulation," *Journal of Political Economy,* vol. 89 (December 1981), pp. 1142–61; and Nancy Peregrim Marion and Lars E. O. Svensson, "Adjustment to Expected and Unexpected Oil Price Changes," *Canadian Journal of Economics,* vol. 17 (February 1984), pp. 15–31, and "World Equilibrium with Oil Price Increases: An Intertemporal Analysis," *Oxford Economic Papers,* vol. 36 (March 1984), pp. 86–102. The model in the appendix to this paper follows Sachs, *Theoretical Issues,* in that the government does all the borrowing but passes the proceeds along to households by adjusting taxes or transfer payments.

36. On these debates, see U.S. Review Committee for Balance of Payments Statistics, *The Balance of Payments Statistics of the United States: A Review and Appraisal* (Government Printing Office, 1965), chap. 9.

37. Some authors straddled these positions. For Meade, trade-related capital flows were "accommodating" and thus served as financing for deficits and surpluses, but capital flows

but rather differently than they were in earlier discussions. I will be dealing mainly with the real side of the economy. In fact, I will not even mention the nominal exchange rate or foreign exchange market. Furthermore, I will be examining the effects of exogenous reductions in domestic output and in the foreign demand for that output. In this context, balance of payments problems will show up as current account surpluses or deficits, and adjustment will involve the elimination of those surpluses and deficits by suitable combinations of income and price effects. But the government will not have to use monetary or fiscal policy to induce adjustment. The requisite changes in aggregate demand and its destination will be brought about endogenously as households and firms react to the exogenous disturbances.

In this framework, moreover, financing can serve only to affect the speed with which adjustment is completed. The economy will not be able to avoid adjustment totally, even when it faces a temporary disturbance. This is because it will be forced to repay any and all borrowing from the outside world and to rebuild its reserves if and when it draws them down. By affecting the speed of adjustment, however, financing can affect the cost of adjustment. When the real wage is rigid in the short run, rapid adjustment can generate unemployment.

I will consider two forms of financing. When the private sector can borrow and lend abroad, it will engage in financing on its own, in the process of optimizing consumption and investment. This is the sort of financing that was sometimes regarded as adjustment in the older literature. When the private sector is unable to borrow or lend, the government can take its place, to optimize consumption and investment on behalf of the private sector or to pursue its own policy objectives. Its borrowing and lending will pass through its budget, by way of changes in taxes or transfers, and will affect the speed of adjustment by affecting private sector behavior. But official financing can also take two forms: borrowing on international capital markets (official financing from private sources) and the use of reserves or reserve credit (official financing from official sources).

Financing by the Private Sector

To identify the reasons for official financing, it is useful to examine first a case in which it may not be needed.

---

induced by interest rate differences were "autonomous" and thus part of the adjustment process; see James E. Meade, *The Balance of Payments* (Oxford University Press, 1951), chaps. 1, 15.

Consider an economy consisting of households that have perfect foresight and firms that produce a single good. The economy is stationary. Firms do not invest, and households do not save, unless they experience fluctuations in their incomes. Households are able to borrow and lend freely on an international capital market, where the interest rate is fixed.[38] They consume the home good and an imported good, which has a fixed foreign currency price. Foreigners consume the home good too, and their demand is not perfectly elastic. In this framework, the real exchange rate is defined by the terms of trade, and the notion of adjustment is associated with changes in that real rate.

Labor is the only variable input used in producing the home good, and wage behavior governs the level of employment. Define the income real wage as the nominal wage deflated by an index of consumer prices that includes the home currency price of the foreign good. If the income real wage is perfectly flexible, a change in the real exchange rate cannot cause unemployment. If the income real wage moves sluggishly, a change in the real exchange rate can cause temporary unemployment, and that is the case considered here.

How will this simple economy respond to an unexpected reduction in the foreign demand for home output? The relative price of the home good will fall immediately (the real exchange rate will depreciate). The effects on output and employment will depend on wage behavior. If the income real wage is perfectly flexible, output and employment will not change. If it is sticky, they will fall temporarily. In both cases, however, households will suffer a reduction in their real incomes, defined in terms of the price index, and will therefore experience a welfare loss.

Having perfect foresight, households will know whether the reduction in foreign demand is permanent or temporary. If it is permanent, the welfare loss will be permanent, and it cannot be deferred by borrowing. Therefore, households will adjust immediately. If the reduction is temporary, the loss will be temporary, and it can be reduced by borrowing abroad to spread out the reduction in consumption required by the temporary fall in income. The appendix to this paper looks at the simplest two-period case, in which households can borrow "today" and repay

38. Formally, households maximize the discounted present value of the utility derived from spending their incomes on home and foreign goods. Their subjective discount rate is equal to the foreign interest rate, and income has diminishing marginal utility. (Perfect foresight is, of course, the nonstochastic equivalent of the rational expectations hypothesis, which asserts that the inhabitants of an economy know all that can be known about its structure, including the government's policy responses to private sector behavior. But it does not preclude surprises of the sort discussed below, which can be regarded as changes in economic structure.)

"tomorrow" to defer part of the cutback in consumption. It shows that they will borrow an amount about equal to half of the fall in foreign demand.

Optimal borrowing of this sort will not keep the real exchange rate from changing. As it will not be large enough to keep consumption constant, it will not prevent a reduction in the households' demand for the home good, let alone offset the exogenous reduction in foreign demand. Therefore, the price of the home good must fall relative to that of the foreign good. In other words, the balance of payments financing provided by optimal private borrowing will take place jointly with adjustment, even when the disturbance inducing it is temporary. With wage stickiness, then, there will be unemployment, though less than there would be if households did not borrow.

Reasons for Official Financing

No economy has the neat properties of the one described above. Goods markets do not clear instantaneously. Households do not have perfect foresight. Even in that idealized context, however, it is easy to adduce reasons for official financing to supplement or substitute for private financing.

Suppose that the government's only policy objective is to maximize its households' welfare as they themselves define it and that the economy confronts a temporary fall in the foreign demand for its exports—a shock that would induce households to borrow. The government will be justified in borrowing if international capital markets discriminate between public and private borrowers. If households are rationed more severely than the government, they may not be able to borrow optimal amounts. If households must pay higher interest rates or repay their debts more quickly, they will not choose to borrow as much and will thus suffer larger welfare losses. In the first case, the government should supplement borrowing by households. In the second, it should substitute for borrowing by households. In both cases, it can pass along the proceeds to households by temporary tax cuts or transfer payments. But households must be made to understand that this fiscal policy change is temporary if it is to have the desired effect—to stretch out a temporary cutback in consumption. In both cases, of course, total borrowing will rise, the households' welfare loss will be reduced, and the change in the real exchange rate will be smaller. There will be more financing and less adjustment.

Official financing will still be justified even if we substitute firms for households. Every borrower's access to credit is constrained by an assessment of its creditworthiness, which depends on its assets, debts, and expected income. But the government's income is apt to be more predictable than the incomes of firms and households, and it has a longer life expectancy. Its income depends chiefly on the national income, which is bound to be more predictable and longer lived than the incomes of individual firms and households, and it can be increased by raising taxes.[39]

There are other reasons for lenders to favor governments. A government can change the terms of access to foreign exchange, including the exchange rate itself, and prevent firms and households from making their debt service payments. Furthermore, it will be seen as a better credit risk because it can be expected to internalize the full costs of a default. When a firm or household cannot meet its obligations, it may not be able to borrow again, but it may also sully the reputations of other firms and households, which will then have to pay higher interest rates or be rationed more severely. Some of the costs of default are external to the firm or household directly involved, and it will not take account of them when making its decisions. When a government fails to meet its obligations, the costs may be even higher; the whole private sector may be cut off, along with the government. But the government is likely to internalize those costs when making its decisions. Therefore, it may try harder to meet its obligations and be regarded as a better credit risk.

Consider next a government that is not concerned exclusively to maximize its households' welfare. It wants to combat the unemployment arising from wage stickiness, even at some cost in terms of household welfare. Optimal private sector borrowing will reduce the amount of unemployment produced by a temporary fall in foreign demand, and unemployment will be reduced even more sharply if the government supplements private sector borrowing. But such borrowing will not prevent unemployment completely, because it will not offset the whole output-reducing effect of a fall in foreign demand. Furthermore, there will be no private sector borrowing when the fall in demand is permanent, but there will still be temporary unemployment if there is wage stickiness.[40] In the simple economy considered here, however, unemployment can be eliminated by deferring adjustment until wage stickiness has worn off, and this furnishes an additional justification for official financing.

39. The power to tax is cited frequently in efforts to explain why governments can borrow more freely than their citizens, and limits on that power may likewise explain why governments run into debt crises; see Sachs, *Theoretical Issues*.

40. There will be no such borrowing, moreover, to deal with certain other disturbances that also lead to temporary unemployment. One such disturbance, an output shock, is examined in the appendix.

Look at the government's role from another standpoint. To stabilize employment in the face of wage stickiness, the government must offset the output-reducing effects of a fall in foreign demand, which can be done by cutting taxes to stimulate domestic consumption. But the government will then run a budget deficit, and that is where official borrowing comes in. By borrowing abroad, the government can cover its budget deficit and can also cover the current account deficit resulting from the fall in foreign demand and policy-induced increase in domestic consumption.

Let us put this argument in general terms. If adjustment is costly in that it causes unemployment but the costs are reduced by slowing down or stretching out the adjustment process, financing should be combined with adjustment, even in the face of a permanent disturbance to which the economy must adapt eventually. But financing can work perversely and raise the costs of adjustment if it ratifies practices and expectations that have to be modified sooner or later. In the case just considered, where unemployment can be eliminated by tax cuts that defer adjustment until wage stickiness wears off, the government must persuade the private sector that the tax cuts are temporary. Otherwise, workers and employers may fail to revise their expectations and will then postpone the permanent reduction in the real wage required by a permanent reduction in foreign demand. Full employment today may be purchased at the expense of unemployment tomorrow.

It is not easy in principle or practice to initiate adjustment promptly—to influence the plans of firms and households—while appearing to resist adjustment by borrowing or drawing down reserves (and resisting it in fact as well as appearance insofar as official financing delays or compresses the price changes that signal the need for firms and households to revise their plans). The problem is compounded by uncertainty. It is not usually possible to observe disturbances directly, and they do not arrive one by one. It is therefore hard to decide whether a disturbance originates at home or abroad, whether it is real or monetary, and whether it is permanent or transitory. Finally, no one knows enough about adjustment costs to declare dogmatically that it is better to err on the side of haste than on the side of procrastination.

Fast adjustment has been in fashion, thanks partly to the appealing doctrine that dramatic policy changes can reduce adjustment costs by causing firms and households to revise their expectations before market forces make them do so. On this view, governments reacted too slowly and timidly to the inflationary pressures stemming from the first oil shock and did much better when they faced the second. But these are debatable conclusions. Could governments have contained the pressures from the first oil shock without inducing a recession even deeper than the one the world experienced in 1974–75? Can good grades be given to policies in 1979–81 without taking account of the recession that followed? How much of the subsequent debt crisis should be blamed on those policies? The record is not clear. In any case, the consensus favoring fast adjustment and minimal financing is biased by one episode, the inflation of the 1970s, just as an earlier consensus favoring slow adjustment and generous financing was biased by another, the depression of the 1930s. Left to themselves, of course, governments are not prone to err on the side of haste in dealing with balance of payments problems, and those who urge them to act quickly may help to keep them from acting too slowly. But that is a second-best reason for giving imperfect advice.

Two reasons have been given for official financing of balance of payments deficits. First, the private sector may not have adequate access to international capital markets. Second, the government may seek to combat unemployment arising from short-run wage stickiness.

The first justification is subject to an important qualification. When the private sector cannot borrow freely, government borrowing can raise economic welfare. To engage in this sort of optimal borrowing, however, the government must be able to replicate the welfare-maximizing calculations of the private sector. It must know what firms and households would borrow if they faced credit conditions no less favorable than those faced by the government.

The second justification, reducing unemployment due to wage stickiness, belongs to a broad class of arguments for official financing that invoke the effects of imperfections and externalities.[41] Another argument belonging to that class deserves brief attention. In the simple economy examined earlier, price changes had immediate effects on the destination of expenditure and thus the current account balance. When those expenditure-switching effects take place with long lags, rapid adjustment can be achieved only by making large cuts in expenditure or making changes in the real exchange rate larger than those needed for long-run equilibrium. In such cases, official financing is required to stretch out the adjustment process and avoid both sorts of overshooting—the making of large expenditure cuts, which lead to large losses of output and employment, and the amplification of changes in relative prices.

41. Unemployment due to wage stickiness is usually said to reflect an imperfection but may be said to reflect an externality. If wage-setting arrangements were designed to internalize all costs, including the costs of unemployment, they might not produce unemployment. But this does not happen, and arrangements that are optimal for some workers are not optimal for others; by protecting some workers' real incomes they jeopardize other workers' jobs.

There is one more justification for official interference with endogenous balance of payments adjustment. Governments may have more or better information than the private sector, information about the state and functioning of the economy and about their own and other governments' intentions.

Many economists say that governments should not act on such information but should make it available to firms and households, because they are more efficient than governments at using information. Two arguments support this view. First, there is an important difference between the information sets available to the public and private sectors. All of the information available to the government can be conveyed to firms and households, in principle if not in practice, but all of the information available to firms and households cannot be conveyed to the government. One set is centralized and fairly small; the other is decentralized and very large. When the government acts on its own, then, it necessarily acts on the basis of *less* information than would be available to firms and households had the government disseminated its information. Second, by distributing information, the government invites a "second opinion" concerning the quality of that information; firms and households are free to accept or reject it. They may sometimes reject it wrongly, but mistakes of this sort are apt to be less costly to the whole economy than those made by the government when it accepts and acts on erroneous information. This, indeed, is the main point. When a single firm or household acts on erroneous information, regardless of source, it bears most of the costs of its mistake. (Not all of the costs in the case of a firm, because its workers are affected, and because large firms affect other firms.) When the government acts on erroneous information, the whole economy bears the costs.

Three arguments oppose the transfer of all information to the private sector and favor official intervention instead. First, information supplied by the government is sometimes tainted by its source. Governments lack credibility, especially with respect to announcements about their own policies. Therefore, firms and households tend to discount the government's forecasts and announcements, regardless of quality. Second, when the government's forecasts and announcements are taken seriously, they can have unwanted side effects. If the government anticipates trouble, a recession perhaps, it can take steps to falsify its own forecast. If it disseminates its forecast, households and firms may react in ways that validate the forecast. Third, information provided by the government is likely to have distributional effects. When firms and households believe what the gov-

30

ernment tells them, those able to do so will position themselves to maximize gains and minimize losses. If they did not, there would be no point in telling them anything. But each bit of news is particularly valuable to certain firms and households, and some can position themselves more advantageously than others. Therefore, governments have reason to fear that they will be accused of favoring certain firms and households, and silence on some matters is the only prudent policy.

The issue is complicated, and dogmatic advice is bound to be wrong. The case for intervention cannot be dismissed.

The Demand for Official Financing

Few points made in the foregoing survey are new, and most have been made many times. But familiar arguments must be repeated and recast, lest they be crowded out by new notions and fashions in theory and policy. Furthermore, the survey has shown that the case for official financing holds up rather well even when households and firms are assumed to behave rationally and have perfect foresight. And when their behavior falls short of this standard, the case for official financing becomes even stronger.

Unfortunately, a survey of this sort gives us no guidance concerning the size of the demand for official financing, let alone the portion that should be accommodated in the interests of the international community. In fact, there is no reliable way to quantify the demand for official financing.

In a paper written when exchange rates were pegged, I suggested that the demand for international reserves might be measured by using short-term changes in reserves to represent exogenous disturbances.[42] But I noted that these changes could not measure disturbances perfectly because "recorded changes in reserves will always reflect the influence of policies initiated to control the nation's balance of payments," and because they can only reflect the distribution of actual disturbances, whereas the demand for reserves must depend on the distribution of future disturbances.[43]

---

42. Peter B. Kenen and Elinor B. Yudin, "The Demand for International Reserves," *Review of Economics and Statistics,* vol. 47 (August 1965), pp. 242–50. Even at that early stage, we used a more sophisticated measure, "whitening" the changes in reserves by an autoregressive scheme. Some would interpret that today as an attempt to distinguish between anticipated and unanticipated disturbances.

43. Kenen and Yudin, "The Demand for International Reserves," p. 246. We also warned that reported reserve changes were not perfect measures of official financing because they did not allow for official borrowing (at that time, mainly drawings on Fund credit and central bank swap lines). The problem is larger now because we do not know how to classify medium-term public sector borrowing or private sector borrowing guaranteed by governments—how much to treat as balance of payments financing.

Faulty as it was, the same technique is still being used, although it is even less appropriate for a world in which exchange rates change frequently.[44] Intervention is more or less mandatory when exchange rates are pegged, and the resulting changes in reserves can be deemed to represent exogenous disturbances, crudely if not perfectly. Intervention is discretionary when exchange rates are flexible, and changes in reserves can represent only those disturbances or portions of disturbances that the authorities have chosen to finance. Therefore, they cannot be used in empirical work unless governments behave with mechanical consistency, and the plausibility of that supposition is challenged by another. A government's choice between financing and adjustment is probably affected by the availability of financing.

Other numbers have been used to measure the need for balance of payments financing, but most of them are flawed. Like changes in reserves, they relate to the past, not the future, and reflect policy decisions that are themselves affected by the availability of financing. Furthermore, they are less comprehensive than changes in reserves. Much attention has been paid in recent years to the evolution of current account balances. But they can move inversely to observable financing. In 1980 and 1981, the current account deficits of the nonoil developing countries added up to $197 billion, yet those countries built up their reserves by $12 billion (net of reserve-credit use). In 1982 and 1983, by contrast, their current account deficits fell to $139 billion, yet they ran down their reserves by $15 billion.[45] The difference was due, of course, to the sharp drop in bank lending and other capital inflows. When capital flows are part of the

44. See, for example, Frenkel, "International Liquidity and Monetary Control," pp. 65–109. Frenkel finds a small but statistically significant shift in the demand for reserves with the change from pegged to floating rates. But the shift is opposite in sign to what one would expect; an increase in the variability of changes in reserves raises the desired stock of reserves by more in the floating rate period than in the pegged rate period. This result may be explained by a point made later in the text; under floating rates, the variability of changes in reserves can measure only a fraction of the variance in the underlying balance of payments shocks. Edwards finds that countries that altered their exchange rates frequently demanded smaller stocks of reserves, a result consistent with the point made in the text. As he observes, however, causality may run the other way; countries with small reserves may be forced to change their exchange rates frequently. See Sebastian Edwards, "The Demand for International Reserves and Exchange Rate Adjustments: The Case of LDCs, 1964–1972," *Economica*, vol. 50 (August 1983), pp. 273–74.

45. International Monetary Fund, *World Economic Outlook*, IMF Occasional Paper 27 (IMF, 1984), pp. 196–97. In both periods, those countries built up their reserves but made extensive use of Fund credit. Countries described by the Fund as "major borrowers" experienced a smaller reduction in their current account deficits, but the difference in their use of reserves was larger. In 1980–81, they built up their reserves and reserve-credit lines by about $1 billion; in 1982–83, they drew them down by $37 billion.

problem, not part of the solution, current account balances do not tell us much about the need for reserves and reserve credit.

We can perhaps expect the demand for financing from official sources to be smaller for the next several years than it was in 1982–83, when the use of Fund credit reached record levels. We can likewise expect the demand for all forms of financing, including new bank credit, to be smaller than it was in 1974–83, a decade which included two oil shocks, two deep recessions, and the onset of large debt problems. We cannot rule out new shocks. The unexpected is virtually inevitable. But governments will probably keep their economies under closer control than they did in the 1970s, opting for more adjustment and less financing. They cannot count on an elastic supply of bank credit but have indeed to worry about perverse movements in supply, because an emerging balance of payments problem is apt to raise questions about creditworthiness.

Nevertheless, it would be imprudent to forecast a steady decline in the demand for official financing during the next decade or to expect the demand to come mainly from those countries that were large users during the last decade. It would be more realistic to expect a drop in demand from recent levels but growth thereafter at a rate no slower than the growth rate of world trade. (This projection assumes that there will be no major change in the exchange rate regime. The move to floating rates in the 1970s did not have a large effect on the demand for reserves, measured by conventional techniques. But a move to more intensive management, let alone to pegging, would probably require a big increase in the supply of financing. An attempt to reduce exchange rate fluctuations would call for close policy coordination among the governments concerned, but it would also call for much larger amounts of official intervention than those that have become customary.)

Before pursuing the implications of these issues for the size and functioning of the International Monetary Fund, I must deal with two other issues. To what extent should the need for official financing be met by borrowing in capital markets and to what extent by drawing on official sources? Should the need for financing from official sources be met by creating reserves or raising the supply of reserve credit?

Comparing the Forms of Financing

Governments can finance balance of payments deficits by drawing down assets or incurring liabilities. But this simple balance-sheet distinction is not very helpful. From the standpoint of a user, forms of financing should be compared in terms of three characteristics: the costs of acquiring and using them; the reliability of access to them; and the obligations that attach to using them.

Costs

A government earns interest on its currency reserves. It does not earn or pay interest on Fund-related reserve assets when its holdings are intact (when its reserve position is equal to one quarter of its quota and its SDR holdings are equal to its cumulative allocation), and it does not pay interest on undrawn access to Fund credit or to other credit lines. But the costs of using these two methods of financing are very similar. When a government draws down its reserves, it sacrifices interest income; when it uses Fund credit or other forms of reserve credit, it has to pay interest. Furthermore, the same opportunity costs attach to the reconstitution of reserves and of reserve-credit lines.

Suppose that a government has used all of its reserves and all of its access to credit in order to finance capital formation. It will earn no interest on reserves and will be making interest payments on its use of credit lines. But these forgone earnings and interest payments will be offset or more than offset by the additional income (output) produced by a larger capital stock. If the government rebuilds its access to balance of payments financing by running down the capital stock to acquire reserves and repay debt, it will increase its interest income and reduce its interest payments, but it will lose some of the income produced by the capital stock. The costs of acquiring access to balance of payments financing will depend on the form of financing; interest rates earned on reserve assets are usually lower than those paid on debts. These differences, however, are apt to be small compared to the difference between the interest income earned or saved and the return on the capital stock. Furthermore, the interest rate differences among the major forms of financing are much smaller than two other differences among them: reliability of access and obligations attaching to their use.

Access

In the matter of reliability of access, the distinction between assets and liabilities is not helpful. If currency reserves have been acquired by running a current account surplus, there can be little question about their

34

subsequent availability. A government can count on having them and using them at its discretion. If the same reserves have been acquired by borrowing, much depends on the manner of the borrowing. Currency reserves obtained by issuing "consols" to foreigners cannot be taken away by a crisis of confidence. Those obtained by issuing debt that has to be rolled over can be taken away just when they are needed. A country that begins to run a current account deficit and looks to finance it by using reserves may find that it must use them to repay debt instead; it cannot roll over its debt because its deficit has frightened its creditors.

Access to Fund-related reserve assets is quite reliable. Reserve positions are acquired initially by paying other reserve assets over to the Fund; they do not represent additions to reserves. Holdings of SDRs reflect allocations initially, and they do represent additions to reserves. Formally, they are the only reserve assets that governments acquire by permanent borrowing; members issue "consols" to the Fund on which they pay interest forever, and they earn interest on their SDR holdings. But reserve positions and SDR holdings can be drawn down at the discretion of the holder.[46] Holdings of both assets are apt to rise when a country runs a balance of payments surplus, but there is a sense in which the availability of these incremental holdings depends on the nature of that surplus. A country that runs a current account surplus "earns" additional Fund-related reserve assets; one that has a capital inflow "borrows" them because it will lose them if the inflow is reversed.

The objection to reliance on borrowed reserves applies with even greater force to reliance on new borrowing once a country has begun to run a balance of payments deficit. Access to quota-based Fund credit is still reliable. In fact, supplies of credit from official sources can display an unexpected elasticity; the SFF and EAP provide examples, as do the bridge loans made to Mexico and other countries at the start of the debt crisis. But access to other forms of credit can exhibit perverse elasticity; supplies can be cut off by the very events that generate the need for them. They can even be cut off by events that have nothing to do with the particular circumstances of the country seeking to use them—the problem of "contagion" that received so much attention in 1982–83. Furthermore, access to new credit can be cut off completely, whereas borrowed reserves can disappear only as fast as old debts mature.

---

46. A member must make a representation of balance of payments need to draw on its reserve position and invoke designation when using SDRs, but that representation cannot be challenged ex ante. Furthermore, we are looking here at availability in precisely such cases of balance of payments need.

Obligations

Two sorts of obligations attach to the use of official financing and distinguish some forms from others. They pertain to repayment or reconstitution and to the user's policies.

When a government uses currency reserves, it does not encumber itself in any formal way. It may want to rebuild its reserves eventually but can decide for itself whether and when to do so. It does not have to modify its economic policies unless and until it decides that the rebuilding of reserves is urgent enough to take priority over other policy objectives.[47] In this respect, of course, Fund-related reserve assets are much like currency reserves; it is no longer necessary to repay drawings on reserve positions, and SDR holdings have not had to be rebuilt since the reconstitution requirement was rescinded in 1981.

Most other forms of financing must be repaid, however, and some are conditional on policy commitments, explicit or implicit.

In the case of Fund credit, both obligations are explicit. Credit tranche drawings must be repaid on schedule, and drawings beyond the first credit tranche carry with them the familiar forms of Fund conditionality. In other cases of financing, the obligations are less clear. Commitments to repay may be explicit, but borrowers and lenders may both expect debt to be rolled over, and debtors may expect this to happen even when creditors do not, because debtors plan to borrow from Peter in order to repay Paul. Such expectations can be disappointed, however, which is what happens in debt crises. The boundary between renewable and nonrenewable debt shifts suddenly, and debts must be rescheduled to put it back in place. For this reason, moreover, governments that borrow heavily in international capital markets may be deemed to be accepting policy conditions similar to those required by the Fund—to be making implicit representations about their future policies in order to maintain creditworthiness and roll over debt in accordance with their own expectations.

This analogy has limited validity, however, because there are large differences between the explicit commitments made to the Fund and the implicit commitments made to other lenders. Those made to the Fund cannot be revised unilaterally. The Fund can change its policies regarding

47. A government may have to modify its policies quickly to halt a loss of reserves, but this merely says that permanent financing is not feasible or optimal. Furthermore, this caveat applies to all forms of financing; it does not distinguish one from another. It is important to distinguish clearly between two policy changes—the one required to stem a loss of reserves by ending a balance of payments deficit and the one required to rebuild reserves by replacing the deficit with a surplus. The distinction is not drawn clearly enough in many discussions of Fund conditionality and will come up again in that context.

access to Fund credit, but once it has approved a standby arrangement, it does not ask a government to adopt stricter standards of conduct than those it approved originally. Commitments required by other lenders can be revised abruptly and, like other judgments made by credit and capital markets, can be altered in ways and for reasons that do not relate directly to the behavior of a particular borrower. Furthermore, the Fund can relax existing policy conditions if it becomes clear that they were unrealistic. Most other lenders are likely to move in the opposite direction—to ask for more strenuous efforts on behalf of creditworthiness when a country's problems either prove to be more serious than seemed to be the case originally or worsen because of a deterioration in external conditions that the country cannot control.

Finally, commitments to the Fund are enforceable only insofar as a government plans to draw more from the Fund. If the government does not live up to them, the Fund can suspend its access to credit but does not change the speed at which earlier drawings must be repaid. If a government does not live up to the implicit commitments it has made to private lenders to maintain creditworthiness, its creditors can refuse to lend it more, just as the Fund can, but they can also refuse to roll over old debt and thus impose repayment terms more onerous than those expected by the borrower. The terms of access to Fund credit are clear and fairly stable; they can be revised periodically, but not without notice and not retroactively. The terms of access to other forms of credit are less clear, can change abruptly, and can change retroactively.

From the standpoint of governments wanting to finance balance of payments deficits, reserve use is better than borrowing in three ways. No one can prevent a government from using its reserves; no one can instruct it to rebuild them; and no one can require it to change its policies.[48] In language used earlier, a government can engage in intertemporal optimization and pursue other policy objectives without external interference. Admittedly, reserves must be acquired before they can be used; they must be earned or borrowed. But the costs of acquiring and holding reserves are not different fundamentally from the costs of keeping credit lines intact.

From a systemic standpoint, by contrast, borrowing may be better than reserve use, and conditionality may be its main advantage. This possibility must be explored before we can conclude that the Fund should supply

48. The appendix to this paper shows the importance of flexibility in decisions about repaying credits and rebuilding reserves. With uncertainty concerning the duration of disturbances, a fixed-term repayment rule interferes with intertemporal optimization; governments cannot make state-contingent decisions about the speed at which they will move into balance of payments surplus.

reserves rather than reserve credit. Two distinct questions must be answered. Is some systemic purpose served by requiring full, prompt repayment (reconstitution) rather than leaving its extent and timing to individual governments? Is some such purpose served by imposing explicit policy conditions on access to balance of payments financing?

These questions do not have unambiguous answers, but the very reasons for ambiguity suggest a strong conclusion. The Fund should provide reserves as well as conditional reserve credit.

The Question of Repayment

Article I of the Fund agreement, listing the purposes of the Fund, commits it "to give confidence to members by making the general resources of the Fund temporarily available to them under adequate safeguards" and "to shorten the duration and lessen the degree of disequilibrium in the international balances of payments of members."

Similar language appears in Article V, sec. 3, governing use of the Fund's resources: "The Fund shall adopt policies on the use of its general resources . . . that will assist members to solve their balance of payments problems in a manner consistent with the provisions of this Agreement and that will establish adequate safeguards for the temporary use of the general resources of the Fund." Thereafter, section 7 sets out the conditions under which a member must repay Fund credit by repurchasing its currency. It is "expected" to do so as its balance of payments and reserve position improve and is required to do so when "the Fund represents to the member that it should repurchase because of an improvement in its balance of payments and reserve position." Furthermore, a member must repurchase its currency "not later than five years after the date on which the purchase was made," and the Fund may require that repurchases be made in installments "during the period beginning three years and ending five years after the date of a purchase."[49]

This last provision, added in 1978, makes the present version of the Fund agreement sharply different from the Keynes and White plans and from the original Fund agreement adopted at Bretton Woods, none of which called for the fixed-term use of the Fund's resources.

49. Article V, sec. 7(b) and (c). Under sec. 7(c) and (d), the Fund may change its time limits, and this authority was used to establish the EFF and lengthen the time limit for repaying borrowed resources under the EAP.

38

Under the original Articles of Agreement, a member was required to repurchase its currency whenever the Fund's holdings came to exceed 75 percent of the member's quota, but the size of the repurchase was tied to the change in the member's reserves during the previous year, and the requirement was overridden if the member's reserves were very low.[50] This approach raised difficulties, however, because it attached great importance to the definition of reserves and interpretations of that definition, and because it could lead to long-lasting use of the Fund's resources. As a matter of policy, then, the Fund began to require repurchase within three to five years after a drawing if an earlier repurchase was not required by the reserve-related rule.[51] When the Fund agreement was amended in 1978, the reserve-related rule was replaced with the more general language quoted earlier, and the five-year rule was added.

The Rationale for Fixed-Term Use

The fixed-term use of Fund resources is usually defended by citing the phrase about "temporary use" in Article V of the Fund agreement and supported by invoking the following three arguments for temporary use. First, every member of the Fund has the right to draw on its resources. Therefore, those resources must be made to revolve by the prompt repayment of all drawings. In language used earlier, the Fund must look to its liquidity if it is to honor the principle of mutuality. Second, the financing of a balance of payments deficit is justified only when the deficit is temporary or when financing will reduce the costs of adjustment. Placing time limits on members' use of Fund credit will make them attentive to this principle. Third, financing involves a transfer of real resources from surplus to deficit countries, and resources should be returned to their owners. This restitution can be effected by making a deficit country repay Fund credit and thus move into balance of payments surplus. Are these three arguments adequate justification for strict fixed-term use of the Fund's resources?

50. The formula required a member to repurchase half of any increase in Fund holdings of its currency during the previous year plus half of any increase in its reserves, and the formula held algebraically. If a member's reserves fell, for example, the reduction was to be deducted from the increase in Fund holdings of its currency, and half of the difference (if positive) was to be repurchased. But the formula was bounded by three conditions: no repurchase was to be carried to a point at which the member's reserves would fall below 150 percent of its quota, the Fund's holdings of its currency would fall below 75 percent of its quota, or the repurchase would be larger than 25 percent of the member's quota.

51. Joseph Gold, *The Second Amendment of the Fund's Articles of Agreement*, IMF Pamphlet Series 25 (IMF, 1978), p. 32.

The first argument is seriously flawed. Three simple examples demonstrate that the fixed-term use of Fund resources may not be necessary or sufficient to protect the Fund's liquidity and make its resources revolve. In the first and second examples, countries must look to the Fund for balance of payments financing; they do not hold reserves.[52] In both of those examples, moreover, the Fund's resources consist entirely of its members' currencies; it does not hold "outside" assets. In the third example, by contrast, the Fund holds and operates in SDRs, and its members hold them too. Exchange rates are pegged in all three examples, which deal with pure financing rather than a mixture of financing and adjustment.

Case I. The world consists of two countries, Britain and France, which have identical quotas in the Fund. Britain runs a balance of payments deficit, so that France must run a surplus, and Britain finances its deficit by drawing its whole quota from the Fund. It uses pounds to purchase francs.

In this very simple case, the Fund's resources will revolve automatically, without requiring repayment to give effect to the principle of mutuality. Suppose that Britain eliminates its deficit (and thus eliminates the French surplus) but does not move on into surplus; it does not accumulate francs, which means that it cannot repurchase its currency from the Fund. If Britain slips back into deficit later, it will be unable to draw again. It has used up its quota, and the Fund has run out of francs. The two constraints are distinct, but both are binding here. If France runs a deficit later, however, it can draw its whole quota. Its quota is intact, and the Fund's holdings of pounds are more than adequate for the purpose.[53]

Before turning to a three-country case, let us modify this one by allowing quotas to differ in size. If the French quota is smaller than the British quota, Britain cannot draw its whole quota initially. The Fund will not have enough francs. Access to the Fund is limited by the composition of its assets or, more basically, by the quota-based ceiling on France's obliga-

52. This assumption is adopted to simplify the exposition and does not restrict the applicability of the conclusions. It is relaxed in the footnotes that amplify the text.

53. If France runs a deficit, Britain must run a surplus, because there are only two countries in this example. Furthermore, Britain *must* repurchase pounds from the Fund, because no country holds currency reserves. What happens when we relax that assumption, allowing Britain to accumulate francs? The Fund's resources will not revolve automatically, but that is not problematical. If Britain accumulates francs, France does not have to draw on the Fund; Britain finances France's deficit. If France prefers to draw on the Fund rather than incur reserve-currency liabilities to Britain, it can still do so; the Fund's holdings of pounds are more than adequate. France can draw pounds and use them to buy francs from Britain or sell them in the foreign exchange market to keep Britain from accumulating francs.

tion to provide financing through the Fund. But repayment is not needed even in this instance. When France begins to run a deficit, it can draw its whole quota, even if Britain has not repurchased pounds. If the French quota is larger than the British quota, Britain can draw its whole quota initially, and France can do so later, but only if Britain does *not* repurchase pounds. A repurchase would keep France from drawing its whole quota by reducing the Fund's holdings of pounds.[54]

Case II. The world consists of three countries, Britain, France, and Japan, which have identical quotas. Britain moves into deficit, France has the corresponding surplus, and Britain draws its whole quota by purchasing francs from the Fund.[55] After the British drawing, the Fund will have pounds and yen but no francs.

In this case, the Fund's resources may not revolve automatically if Britain does not repurchase pounds and thus restore the Fund's holdings of francs. If Britain eliminates its deficit but does not run a surplus, Britain cannot draw again, because it has used up its quota. France can draw its whole quota if it runs a deficit; the Fund's holdings of yen are equal to the Japanese quota and thus equal to the French quota, and its holdings of pounds are larger than the French quota. But Japan's situation is different. It can draw its whole quota if it runs a deficit but can only draw pounds, since the Fund has no francs.

This limitation poses no problem when Britain has the surplus corresponding to the Japanese deficit. It poses a serious problem when France has that surplus, because Japan must be able to draw francs.[56] And the problem is not necessarily solved by requiring Britain to repurchase pounds before Japan moves into deficit. The outcome depends on the

---

54. Because Britain is the first to draw in this example, it incurs an extra obligation to provide financing if it does not repurchase its currency, and this makes it possible for France to draw its whole quota later, although its quota is larger than Britain's quota. If Britain had repurchased its currency, it would have discharged that extra obligation and made it impossible for France to draw its whole quota.

55. Britain could purchase yen to finance its deficit; it could sell them for pounds in the foreign exchange market to keep the pound from depreciating. But the yen would then tend to depreciate in terms of the franc, and Japan would have to sell francs for yen. As Japan does not hold currency reserves in this example, it would have to use yen to buy francs from the Fund. The Fund would wind up with yen and pounds but no francs, and the three countries' positions would be the same as they are in the text.

56. For reasons made clear in the previous footnote, Japan must be able to draw francs when France has the surplus. If it drew pounds and sold them to support the yen, the pound would tend to depreciate in terms of the franc, and Britain could not support it. It has used up its Fund quota, and it could not draw francs anyway, because the Fund does not have them. Similar reasoning explains why the Fund must insist that Britain use francs when and if it repurchases pounds; the Fund must rebuild its holdings of francs to be able to finance a future drawing by Japan occasioned by a Japanese deficit and French surplus.

country that moves into deficit when Britain moves into surplus in order to repurchase its currency. If France moves into deficit, the problem is solved completely. In fact, the repurchase is not strictly necessary; as France must use francs to buy pounds from the Fund, its purchase will raise the Fund's holdings of francs and reduce its holdings of pounds, making the British repurchase redundant. If Japan moves into deficit when Britain moves into surplus, the problem remains. Japan moves into deficit vis-à-vis Britain before it develops its subsequent deficit vis-à-vis France. It must draw on the Fund to finance that first deficit and cannot finance the second, because it has used up its quota.[57]

On close inspection, however, the problem facing Japan and the Fund turns out to reflect the tendency for France to run surpluses without having to provide adequate financing for them. It had the surplus corresponding to the British deficit with which this example began, as well as the one corresponding to the subsequent Japanese deficit that poses the problem for Japan and the Fund. Furthermore, Britain's repurchase of pounds cannot solve the problem when the requisite British surplus is matched by a Japanese deficit, and the repurchase is redundant when the British surplus is matched by a French deficit. If France were willing or required to lend francs to the Fund, however, Japan could draw its whole quota without any repurchase by Britain. This point is underscored by one more example.

Case III. The Fund starts with SDRs rather than national currencies and sells them for national currencies whenever its members make drawings.[58] Thus, Britain buys SDRs when it runs a deficit and sells them to

57. If Japan buys pounds from the Fund to finance the first deficit, Britain does not have to repurchase them. But Japan will use up its quota, and the Fund will wind up with fewer pounds and more yen but will not acquire francs. (The effect on the Fund is important for understanding what happens in a world with four or more countries. Replace Japan with Italy and Spain, and suppose that Italy runs a deficit when Britain moves into surplus. Italy will draw pounds from the Fund, and the Fund will wind up with more lire, fewer pounds, and no francs. Italy cannot draw again because it has used up its quota. But Spain is also prevented from drawing francs when it runs a deficit vis-à-vis France, even though it has not drawn before, as the Fund has been unable to replenish its holdings.)

58. Arrangements of this sort are discussed at more length in the final section of this paper. This example differs from those above in that members hold reserves (SDRs), but this difference does not alter the continuity of the argument. If reserves were introduced into earlier examples, they would complicate the story but not change it fundamentally. Returning to the three-country example, suppose that Britain moves into surplus after running a deficit, driving France into deficit, and that Britain accumulates francs instead of repurchasing pounds from the Fund. The situation is similar to the one in the text. The Fund can finance drawings by France and Japan if they require pounds but cannot finance a drawing by Japan if it requires francs. In this instance, however, the Fund could sell pounds to Japan, which could invoke Article V, sec. 3(e), of the Fund agreement, under which Britain must

France, the surplus country, to obtain the francs needed for intervention to support the pound. This initial transaction will not exhaust the Fund's ability to accommodate drawings by other members. It can have this effect indirectly, however, if France reaches its acceptance limit, which becomes the ceiling on France's obligation to provide financing through the Fund.

There will be no problem if France is the next country to run a deficit. It can draw its whole quota from the Fund or use its own holdings of SDRs. In both cases, it can sell SDRs to the surplus country (unless that country had reached its own acceptance limit before this example started). If Japan is the next deficit country, however, and France is the corresponding surplus country, Japan and the Fund will face the old problem. Japan can draw SDRs from the Fund but cannot sell them to France (and it would serve no purpose to sell them to Britain).

As before, the problem will be solved if Britain repurchases pounds from the Fund, runs the necessary surplus in its balance of payments, and drives France into deficit. As before, moreover, the repurchase is not really necessary.[59] But the problem will not be solved if the British surplus drives Japan into deficit.

Summing up, Fund resources will revolve, with or without repayments, when surpluses and deficits revolve. But when one country tends to run surpluses persistently or fails to run deficits when others run surpluses, the Fund's resources cannot revolve, even when repayments are required. That is why the founders of the Fund included the Scarce Currency Clause (Article VII) in the Fund agreement.

Repayment as a Form of Conditionality

The second argument for temporary use, that balance of payments deficits should be financed only when they are temporary or when financing reduces the costs of adjustment, was set out earlier. When forward-looking firms and households believe that a balance of payments deficit is due to a permanent disturbance, they will adjust to it as quickly as possible, and governments should not slow down the process unless they can

---

stand ready to sell its francs for the pounds that Japan has purchased from the Fund. The existence of reserve-currency holdings can actually enhance the liquidity of the Fund, and repurchases become even less important than they were in the two examples from which such holdings were excluded.

59. If Britain undertakes to make the repurchase, it will accumulate francs, use them to buy SDRs from France, and sell the SDRs to the Fund. If it does nothing, France must sell SDRs to Britain to acquire pounds for supporting the franc. In both cases, French holdings of SDRs will fall below the French acceptance limit, paving the way for Japan to draw SDRs from the Fund and sell them to France for francs.

reduce adjustment costs. Time limits on the use of Fund credit, however, may not be a good way to uphold that principle.

When the repayment requirement is used to influence a government's choice between financing and adjustment, it becomes an instrument of conditionality—a way of affecting the government's policies. The arguments for conditionality will be examined shortly and one will be rejected. The Fund should not function in loco parentis, substituting its judgment about the nature of its members' problems for the judgments of the members themselves. It is especially hard to decide early on whether a balance of payments problem will be permanent and thus to justify a particular choice between financing and adjustment.

Furthermore, the fixed-term use of Fund credit is too blunt an instrument for influencing national policies. It substitutes an arbitrary five-year period for the one that the member or Fund would choose in the light of available information. Indeed, it goes much farther. It does not merely limit the duration of a deficit. It says that a surplus must follow every deficit—and forces the pace at which that must happen. Even when we can say with confidence that a country should finance a deficit for one or two years, not longer, we are not necessarily justified in saying that it should run a surplus two or three years later, in order to repay the Fund. This may not be appropriate from the country's standpoint or that of the world as a whole. A government that has just ended a balance of payments deficit may want to pause before it seeks a surplus, especially when it has had to incur high adjustment costs. In some cases, moreover, deficit countries can damage others by moving into surplus.

Suppose that all countries start out in "internal" and "external" balance; economic activity is high and inflation rates are low, and no country is running a balance of payments deficit. When one large country, call it the United States, slips into recession, its imports will fall, and other countries will move into current account deficit. The Fund was created to deal with this sort of situation, in which financing is thoroughly appropriate. By drawing on Fund credit, deficit countries can ride out the U.S. recession; ideally, they can maintain internal balance (but will then have to finance larger current account deficits). When the recession is over, however, and all countries return to internal and external balance, the principle of fixed-term use requires the repayment of Fund credit, and countries that used it during the recession must run surpluses. They must therefore reduce activity at home, which will tend to reduce it in the United States, and this outcome is not optimal from any country's standpoint.[60]

60. They could allow their currencies to depreciate instead, in which case the requisite reductions in expenditure would not necessarily reduce activity. When we admit that possi-

44

More generally, strict application of the repayment rule can destabilize the international economy. When policy instruments affecting flows such as the balance of payments are regulated by the behavior of stocks such as reserve levels or Fund positions, not by the behavior of the flows themselves, the policy instruments and whole economy can exhibit large oscillations.[61]

Returning Real Resources

The final argument for temporary use, that real resources should be returned from deficit to surplus countries, looks behind the use of credit to flows of goods and services. It says that a country financing a balance of payments deficit is laying claim to other countries' real resources. If it could not finance its deficit, it would have to reduce its use of other countries' goods and services by limiting its imports (or make more of its own resources available to others by expanding its exports). Such resource transfers, it is said, should be temporary. The resources belong to the countries providing them and should be returned to their owners. Therefore, deficit countries should be made to run surpluses.[62]

---

bility, however, we abandon the basic principle that temporary disturbances should be financed; if other countries had allowed their currencies to depreciate during the U.S. recession, they would not have needed Fund credit. It may be objected that this whole argument is too Keynesian. But severe recessions are also Keynesian; they would not occur in a world with perfectly flexible prices and rational expectations, even with large policy surprises. (The force of the example *is* diminished by introducing capital mobility. Suppose that current and capital accounts are both balanced before the U.S. recession. When the recession begins, its current account will move into surplus, but the capital account will move into deficit because the recession will reduce U.S. interest rates. Let the capital outflow be larger than the current account surplus, so that the United States runs a balance of payments deficit and draws on the Fund. When the U.S. recession ends, the current account will move back into balance, but the capital outflow will give way to an inflow as U.S. interest rates rise to their prerecession level. The U.S. balance of payments will move into surplus temporarily, and the United States can repay its drawing on the Fund without manipulating domestic activity or adjusting its policy mix to attract a capital inflow.)

61. Peter B. Kenen, "Floats, Glides, and Indicators: A Comparison of Methods for Changing Exchange Rates," *Journal of International Economics,* vol. 5 (May 1975), pp. 107–51.

62. The validity of this argument is not impaired by introducing capital mobility. Suppose that a capital outflow leads to a balance of payments deficit. If adjustment involves an improvement of the current account balance, the argument in the text holds without modification; adjustment requires a cut in imports, a rise in exports, or a combination of the two. If adjustment involves a reduction in the capital outflow, it entails a reduction in the deficit country's claims on other countries' future output. In either case, financing allows the deficit country to use more of the world's resources, now or in the future, than if it had adjusted immediately.

This doctrine is based on an analogy. When a single household saves, it does not consume all of the output attributable to it, releasing resources for others to use. It will not save, however, unless it is free to dissave later on. If countries were like households and had the same objectives, the analogy might hold and validate the argument for temporary use. But it is undermined by the paradox of thrift.

When a single household saves, it does not affect its own income, because it does not affect other households' incomes. When a country saves, by contrast, it affects its income, and it can affect other countries' incomes. This introduces the possibility of slack in the world economy, a possibility neglected by those who argue that transfers of resources should always be reversed. That doctrine assumes that a temporary transfer of goods and services requires a reduction in absorption (consumption or investment) by the country providing them and a subsequent reduction in absorption by the country returning them. This is not true when resources are idle. A deficit country can consume more goods and services without necessarily forcing others to forgo them.

The same point was made above in a different way. When the United States is in recession, real resources go to waste; they are not stored for future use. Therefore, other countries can run current account deficits without any sacrifice by the United States. In fact, those deficits will raise aggregate demand in the United States, reducing its own wastage of resources. In such circumstances, the United States has no reason to insist that resources be returned.

Governments that tell deficit countries to return the real resources supplied by surplus countries do not always honor their own doctrine. They frequently refuse to accept the resources to which they lay claim in principle. They urge deficit countries to move into surplus but are not willing to move into deficit. The same problem was encountered in earlier examples, where Britain had to run a surplus in order to repurchase pounds but France did not run a deficit, and the Fund's resources did not revolve.

When governments say one thing and do another, they should be told that they are being inconsistent. But such reminders are not likely to make them abandon their insistence on fixed-term use of Fund resources. It would therefore be silly to regard repeal of the present five-year rule as an urgent issue. It is more important to make sure that the Fund can supply an adequate amount of balance of payments financing. A small Fund would be worse than one that continued to require fixed-term use, and governments may not consent to growth in the Fund's resources if the rules governing use of those resources are liberalized in ways that offend their views about the obligations of deficit countries.

It may nevertheless be prudent for the Fund to plan on more flexible administration of the present repayment rule. In the next few years, many countries must repay large drawings on the Fund. The stock of Fund credit outstanding on June 30, 1985, was as follows (in billions of SDRs):[63]

Credit tranche drawings	14.3
Ordinary resources	5.5
Borrowed resources	8.8
Extended Fund facility	13.1
Ordinary resources	6.5
Borrowed resources	6.6
Compensatory financing and buffer stock facilities	7.6
Total	35.0

Most of this money must be repaid before the end of the decade, and repayments of Fund credit will figure prominently in total debt service payments due from many countries, because many of their other debts have been rescheduled. The Fund could exacerbate the debt problem instead of helping to solve it.

The Question of Conditionality

The question of conditionality is even more complicated than the question of repayment, for it raises problems of measurement as well as issues of principle.

It is virtually impossible to measure the effectiveness of conditionality. The debate on that subject will continue, because the participants do not agree on the ways in which policy instruments work, and because they cannot know what governments would have done if they had not made policy commitments to the Fund. John Williamson would measure the Fund's success by "the improvement . . . in economic performance in the actual outcome, as opposed to the situation that would have occurred without Fund involvement, as a proportion of the *potential* improvement from [that situation] . . . to the best *potentially* feasible outcome."[64] To make this measurement, we would have to know the whole set of political and other constraints affecting policy selection in a particular country and

63. IMF, *International Financial Statistics,* August 1985, p. 24.
64. John Williamson, "On Judging the Success of IMF Policy Advice," in Williamson, ed., *IMF Conditionality,* p. 132 (emphasis added).

the whole structure of its economy. Otherwise, we would not be able to identify the policies required for the best potentially feasible outcome.

It is not necessary here, however, to measure the success of conditionality as practiced by the Fund. It will suffice to examine the arguments advanced on behalf of the principle, to decide whether there are valid reasons for believing that the Fund should attempt to influence its members' policies.

The Rationale for Conditionality

Three arguments are commonly advanced on behalf of conditionality. First, the Fund must protect its own liquidity by making sure that its members repay Fund credit. Second, the Fund has more information and experience than any single government and can therefore give policy advice that promotes the interests of the individual member that seeks to use Fund credit. Third, the Fund can take account of externalities and other systemic effects that members tend to disregard when making their own policies and can therefore give policy advice that promotes the interests of its members collectively. The first argument is the oldest.[65] The second is heard and criticized most often. The third is the strongest.

Conditionality and Repayment

The first argument rests on the supposition that the Fund's liquidity requires the repayment of Fund credit, a supposition that has already been examined and challenged. The Fund's resources will not revolve unless balance of payments surpluses revolve; repayments are redundant when they do and unhelpful when they don't. Furthermore, conditionality is not an effective way to ensure repayment. The leverage it provides lasts only as long as a member has undrawn access to Fund credit (a standby arrangement in force). After access is exhausted, the Fund cannot compel a member to live up to its commitments. This objection applies, of course, to all of the arguments for conditionality. Commitments are worthless if they are not honored. But it applies most forcefully to this particular

65. On the history of conditionality, see Sidney Dell, *On Being Grandmotherly: The Evolution of IMF Conditionality,* Essays in International Finance 144 (Princeton University, International Finance Section, 1981), and Adolpho C. Diz, "The Conditions Attached to Adjustment Financing: Evolution of the IMF Practice" (and the subsequent "Discussion" by Edwardo Weisner) in *The International Monetary System: Forty Years After Bretton Woods,* pp. 214–43.

argument, which is concerned with safeguarding the interests of the Fund as an institution rather than those of its members, either individually or collectively.

Conditionality and National Policy

The second argument focuses on the role of the Fund in a member's own policymaking and raises questions about information, accountability, and flexibility.

The Fund may have more experience than any government, but it cannot be expected to have more information. It may know more about the international economy because of its ability to gather and integrate information from many governments. It is not likely to know more about each national economy. In this particular context, moreover, a strong case can be made for sharing information and experience rather than imposing policy conditions based on "superior" information. On the basic premise of the argument, that the Fund is concerned with the interests of its members taken individually, information from the Fund would not be tainted by its source.

For the sake of argument, however, suppose that the Fund knows more than any member but can impart its wisdom only by imposing policy conditions on its members' access to Fund credit—that governments, like children, are deaf to the voice of experience and must be told what to do. Should the Fund act in loco parentis?

Parental authority is based on two premises. First, children do not have enough knowledge and experience to forecast the effects of their conduct. Second, children do not always know what is good for them; they cannot be trusted to make sound decisions even when they can predict the effects. Children never grow up in the eyes of their parents; they are never old enough to be trusted completely. At some point, however, they claim the right to make their own mistakes, and society grants it. Governments may sometimes act like children by refusing to face the implications of their own decisions, and the Fund is entitled to give them frank assessments of their policies and prospects. In matters pertaining exclusively to their own welfare, however, the Fund must treat its members as adults. Governments must have the right to make their own mistakes, as they alone are accountable to their citizens.

In the family, moreover, parents can be flexible. They can make decisions on a case-by-case basis, and tailored to the circumstances of each child, without the need to justify every departure from the appearance of uniform treatment. Children complain about "unequal" treatment, but they rarely win the argument. The Fund does not have this much flexibility. It does not have to ask each user of Fund credit to swallow the same medicine, and it does differentiate among broad classes of problems. The CFF, EFF, and oil facilities were set up for this purpose. But it cannot depart sharply from the appearance of uniform treatment to treat each case wholly on its merits. Governments are very sensitive to "unequal" treatment, and the Fund is not free to ignore their complaints. It is ruled by its wards.

The need for flexibility would be much greater if, as is frequently recommended, members came to the Fund "at an early stage" in their balance of payments problems. It would be harder for the Fund to diagnose its members' problems at an early stage, to choose the right mix of financing and adjustment, and harder to select appropriate policies. In some instances, the Fund would want to err on the side of financing, rather than requiring rapid adjustment, and this is difficult under current practices, because conditionality becomes more rigorous as members draw more heavily on the Fund's resources.

Those who would keep governments on a "short leash" to force them into early drawings and confront them quickly with conditionality do not always recognize this difficulty—or they choose to ignore it. But the Fund is thoroughly aware of it. Its guidelines on conditionality do not call on members to make early drawings. They say instead that members should be encouraged at an early stage "to adopt corrective measures, which *could be* supported by use of the Fund's general resources in accordance with the Fund's policies," and they cite the regular consultations between the Fund and its members as "occasions on which the Fund would be able to discuss with members adjustment programs, including corrective measures, that would enable the Fund to approve a stand-by arrangement."[66] In effect, the Fund distinguishes clearly between early use of Fund credit, which might tax its ability to exercise flexibility in judging a member's prospects and policies, and early consultations to facilitate the subsequent use of Fund credit once it becomes clear that a member has an obdurate payments problem for which the appropriate remedies are fairly uniform. This distinction is crucial.

Conditionality and Culpability

Some critics of the Fund charge it with a particular form of inflexibility, asserting that it does not differentiate sufficiently between a payments

66. IMF, *Annual Report, 1979*, pp. 136–37 (emphasis added). The meaning of this passage is not altogether clear; it can be read to say that members should enter into standby arrangements and thus submit to conditionality before they expect to use Fund credit.

problem caused by a country's own policies and one caused by forces beyond its control. They want the Fund to exercise more flexibility, not on the basis of forward-looking judgments about the gravity of a country's problem but of backward-looking judgments about the origins of that problem. This view confuses a submission to conditionality with an admission of culpability. A pedestrian disabled by a drunken driver must adjust to his disability. A country innocent of policy errors cannot escape the need for painful measures when it confronts a deterioration in its terms of trade, an increase in the interest rate on its external debt, or some other exogenous shock likely to last for a long time.

The pedestrian is entitled to compensation for the costs of adjusting to his disability. A country injured by another country's policies might likewise be entitled to compensation if it could prove that the other country had been negligent. Unfortunately, there are no procedures for this purpose, other than those in the General Agreement on Tariffs and Trade (GATT), which deal with clearly defined trade policy actions, and it would be hard to write workable rules of evidence. Who is to blame for the increase in interest rates that helped to produce recent debt problems? One could perhaps bring charges against the United States, but the United States would have a good defense—that the Federal Reserve was responding to inflationary pressures in the best way possible and was not solely responsible for those pressures. To establish culpability, it would be necessary to explain the whole history of the international economy in order to locate those policy errors for which there were no plausible excuses and to decide on appropriate compensation. In the end, moreover, the innocent would still have to adjust to their disabilities.

The Fund may not have enough flexibility to treat individual members according to their circumstances. Insofar as it can be flexible, however, it should be concerned with its members' prospects rather than with attempts to distinguish victims from villains.

Conditionality and National Politics

As a practical matter, conditionality enables the Fund to be helpful to member nations in managing their own affairs. The Fund can both help governments take difficult decisions and persuade the outside world that those decisions will stick. These possibilities are mentioned frequently, but their importance is not fully appreciated.

The Fund is sometimes described as the scapegoat for decisions that governments must take but do not have the courage or political support to take on their own. Governments have used the Fund this way, but not wisely. By blaming the Fund for bad news, governments pander to xenophobia and admit to weakness in the face of external pressure. They lose legitimacy and thus the ability to mobilize domestic political support for their policies.[67]

The Fund can make a different, more constructive contribution during the process of policy formation. Governments are not monolithic, and those officials who must deal with balance of payments problems do not always win their bureaucratic battles. In fact, they are handicapped because they are concerned with the external side of economic policy and do not have strong political constituencies. The Fund can help them during the policymaking process by giving them justification for proposing painful measures and by raising their resistance to pressures for compromise.

Conditionality attaches to the promise of additional financing from the Fund, which countries with large balance of payments deficits need badly. Without it, they confront the need to take measures even harsher than those that will satisfy the Fund. As ministers of finance and governors of central banks represent their governments in dealings with the Fund, their own "seal of approval" on a policy package is essential for access to financing from the Fund, and they carry more weight in their own countries' councils than they would if they could not invoke the Fund's authority and the promise of Fund credit.

The Fund's authority is enhanced by its other role—to assist in convincing the outside world that national policies are firm and credible. When the Fund sets its "seal of approval" on a member's policies and provides financing from its own resources, it can make more financing available from others, including official and commercial institutions. This was its most important contribution during the first phase of the debt crisis.[68] At that point, indeed, the Fund went farther. It imposed "conditionality" on commercial banks by making the commitment of its own resources contingent on the banks' commitment to make new loans and reschedule old loans.

67. On these issues, see Joan M. Nelson, "The Politics of Stabilization," in R.E. Feinberg and V. Kalleb, eds., *Adjustment Crisis in the Third World* (Washington, D.C.: Overseas Development Council, 1984).

68. This role of the Fund has received much attention recently, but it is not new. Per Jacobsson, managing director of the Fund, observed in 1959 that "when a country is clearly in such an unbalanced position that radical measures are required to restore equilibrium, private banks may properly be deterred by the risks involved in granting it further credit facilities. In such situations, it is only if a comprehensive program is adopted and put into effect that the risk will be reduced; and private institutions are not in a position to negotiate such programs. Experience has shown that the Governments in the various countries are more willing to discuss and work out stabilization programs with officials of the Fund than with representatives of other countries or of private credit institutions." IMF, *International Financial News Survey,* vol. 11 (April 10, 1959), p. 315.

The Fund cannot go that far in ordinary circumstances. If banks come to expect that they will be dragooned into additional lending when they would prefer to reduce their exposure, they will avoid exposure from the start and limit the level of international lending. Furthermore, such activism poses risks to the Fund. It is exposed to powerful pressures at times of international financial crisis, and it may be obliged to confer its seal of approval on policies that have little likelihood of success—not even much chance of implementation. When those policies fail, moreover, the Fund faces a dilemma. If it cuts a member off, particularly one that has large debts, it may precipitate a crisis of confidence. If it fails to cut the member off or agrees too readily to modifications in the country's policies, it may tarnish its seal of approval.

Finally, the Fund runs the risk of adapting its own standards to those of other institutions. It is in danger of attaching too much weight to bankers' standards of creditworthiness and too little weight to other desiderata pertaining to the optimal speed of adjustment, the proper choice between cutting and switching expenditure, and the need for the long-term policy reforms described as "structural adjustment." What sorts of policy commitments would the Fund have endorsed during the debt crisis of 1982–83 if its own resources and its members' drawing rights had been large enough for members to dispense with additional bank loans? The question is well worth pondering.

These caveats do not derogate from the importance of the Fund's catalytic role. They warn against stressing it too heavily, rather than financing by the Fund itself.

Conditionality and the Collective Interest

The role of the Fund in dealing with crises of confidence leads us to the third argument for conditionality—safeguarding the collective interests of its members. The Fund's intervention in the debt crisis and the unprecedented steps it took reflected a belief by governments and the Fund's own management that the international financial system was at risk—that the crisis would spread from debtor to debtor and undermine confidence in the banks themselves, with worrisome implications for the functioning of the monetary systems in the major industrial countries and of international financial markets. By imposing conditionality on some of its members, the Fund sought to restore confidence and thus to protect the interests of all members.

There are other, less dramatic ways in which the Fund can use conditionality to safeguard the collective interests of its members. These have to

53

do with the three ways in which one country's policies impinge on other countries' interests.

First, certain policy instruments are common property. There is only one exchange rate connecting two currencies, and it cannot be said to "belong" to a single country. Most trade policy measures belong to this same category, although we do not often think of them that way. In a two-country world, one country's import tariff would have trade and price effects identical to those of an equal export tariff levied by the other country.[69] Asymmetries arise in the real world because the third-country effects of an import tariff differ from those of an export tariff, but the global effects are similar enough to sustain the principle.

Second, trade and capital controls are just as damaging to global efficiency when they are used for balance of payments purposes as when they are used to protect domestic industries or to capture welfare gains along optimal-tariff lines. They reduce the total gains from trade in goods and assets. Furthermore, they can incite retaliation, which leads to larger welfare losses for the world as a whole.

Third, measures that reduce aggregate demand in a deficit country tend to reduce activity in other countries. All of them do so directly, by reducing other countries' exports; the recent fall in U.S. exports to Latin America, especially to Mexico, is a timely illustration. But some measures also do this indirectly; tight monetary policies, for example, tend to drive up interest rates on international capital markets and thus depress investment in all countries that have contact with those markets.

No country can adjust without affecting others, and the larger the country, the larger are the foreign repercussions of its policies. But some costs are avoidable in principle, because they represent resort to second-best policy instruments, and the Fund must try to keep those costs down. It must concern itself with the global impact of each member's policies and with the particular policies adopted. For this last purpose, moreover, the Fund cannot merely reject stabilization programs that rely on second-best policy instruments, such as import restrictions. It must satisfy itself that programs acceptable in form are also adequate in scope. Otherwise, members will be tempted to use second-best policies later. The Fund may therefore appear to be acting paternalistically even when it is mainly concerned with the systemic effects of its members' policies.

---

69. The trade and price effects of the two measures would differ only if the governments had different spending patterns. If the first country's government spent more of its revenue on its own export good, an import tariff by that country would raise the price of that good by more (and reduce the quantity traded by less) than an export tariff by the second country.

It may be appropriate for the Fund to go farther—not merely to engage in damage limitation but also to induce users of Fund credit to contribute to the general objectives of its members. Richard Cooper has suggested that the Fund should vary the terms of conditionality in a contracyclical manner: they should be eased in periods of worldwide recession and tightened in periods of worldwide inflation.[70] In certain circumstances, moreover, conditionality might be used to improve the effectiveness of policy coordination among the major industrial countries and to reduce the frequency of second-best policy outcomes.[71]

Members of the Fund have accepted formally an obligation to conduct their national policies in ways consistent with the interests of others. Under Article IV, sec. 1, of the Fund agreement, each member "undertakes to collaborate with the Fund and other members to assure orderly exchange arrangements and to promote a stable system of exchange rates," and its obligations are defined very broadly. Each member shall:

> (i) endeavor to direct its economic and financial policies toward the objective of fostering orderly economic growth with reasonable price stability, with due regard to its circumstances;
> (ii) seek to promote stability by fostering orderly underlying economic and financial conditions and a monetary system that does not tend to produce erratic disruptions;
> (iii) avoid manipulating exchange rates or the international monetary system in order to prevent effective balance of payments adjustment or to gain an unfair competitive advantage over other members. . . .

But these obligations apply to all members at all times, not just to those that need Fund credit. Furthermore, most of the Fund's clients are small countries and cannot do much damage to other countries' interests. There have been only four credit tranche drawings by major industrial countries since 1968, two by the United Kingdom, and one each by France and

---

70. Richard N. Cooper, "Comment," in Williamson, ed., *IMF Conditionality*, p. 574. Applying Cooper's criterion, Williamson charges that the Fund's policies have been perverse in recent years because conditionality was tightened in 1981, when the world was moving into recession. (Williamson, "The Lending Policies of the International Monetary Fund," in Williamson, ed., *IMF Conditionality*, pp. 640–48.) It can be argued, however, that the Fund was reflecting faithfully its members' own priorities; they had put the fight against inflation ahead of recovery and were willing to endure a sharp recession to turn back inflationary pressures. Polak concurs in Williamson's judgment about the tightening of conditionality in 1981 but endorses the tightening strongly, and he does not agree with Cooper's recommendation; see Polak, "Role of the Fund," pp. 251, 254. (His objections might also apply to recommendations made later in this paper.)

71. See the survey by Richard N. Cooper, "Economic Interdependence and Coordination of Economic Policies," in Jones and Kenen, eds., *Handbook in International Economics*, vol. 2, pp. 1195–1234.

Italy. (The United States drew on its reserve position but did not use Fund credit.) Furthermore, countries that are large enough to justify worldwide concern about their policies are the ones least likely to draw on the Fund in amounts that would expose them to conditionality. They have large reserves and access to other credit facilities, such as those of the European Monetary System. Finally, they have been willing to accept large exchange rate changes rather than engage in official financing on a scale that might force them to turn to the Fund.

In 1982–83, of course, Fund credit was used by a number of medium-sized countries large enough together to influence events in the outside world. Many observers warned that the Fund-approved policies of Mexico, Brazil, and other major debtors could weaken the recovery in the industrial countries and could also interfere with one another, because each country would reduce its imports from the rest. Even in these instances, however, the Fund was not free to exercise much flexibility. It could not have softened its terms in order to avoid damaging others because of the urgency of the countries' problems, the threat to confidence in the banks, and the views of the governments that were the Fund's main partners in the attempt to manage the debt crisis.

The Future of the Fund

When an institution is working well, it should be allowed to find ways around its own rules and conjure up fresh precedents to deal with new problems. Untidiness is not reason enough for revising its constitution. The Fund is working rather well, and major reforms are not urgent. Nevertheless, trends and problems may call for significant changes in the way it works. Before making specific recommendations, I collate the main premises, projections, and conclusions that lead to those recommendations.

Reviewing the Argument

When the Fund was founded, governments were strongly committed to the building of international institutions. Nevertheless, they circumscribed the powers of the Fund and their obligations to it. It was not to be a bank capable of creating international money on a significant scale. It was to be a credit union in which members would have limited rights and obligations.

Governments today are much less interested in building international institutions and are more protective of their sovereignty. It is therefore unrealistic to base proposals for reform on a more ambitious model—to talk of converting the Fund into an international central bank or giving it extensive discretionary access to international capital markets. In fact, the Fund has been reducing its reliance on borrowed resources. It may have to borrow again during the next several years, but mainly to replenish its liquidity in the short term rather than enlarge its lending over the medium term. It is more likely to use the GAB than ad hoc arrangements of the sort that financed most of its lending in the 1970s.[72]

It is equally unrealistic to propose reforms that ignore the views of governments about conditionality. In Richard Cooper's words:

> The IMF is in the business of lending money, and that issue concerns not just the prospective debtors, but also the prospective creditors. If the IMF is to grow with the world economy, the potential creditors have to be satisfied that their interests—and here I mean their conception of the global interest, not merely their national interests—are being served. *Ipso facto,* that will require conditions on IMF lending.[73]

Governments will continue to insist that much of the financing they supply through the Fund be provided on a fixed-term, conditional basis.

Nevertheless, the use of Fund-related reserve assets—drawings on reserve positions and SDR holdings—involves financing through the Fund, and governments do not insist on fixed-term conditional use of these assets. Drawings on reserve positions are not subject to conditionality and do not have to be repaid; holdings of SDRs do not have to be reconstituted even when they have been drawn down with the help of designation. It should be possible, moreover, to introduce more flexibility into the administration of conditionality and of the repayment rule.

Governments will not give the Fund enough flexibility to treat each member's situation wholly on its merits—and the Fund's management may not want it. Members will continue to demand an appearance of uniform treatment even when their circumstances differ. Accordingly, it is important for the Fund to apply conditionality at points in the development of a member's problem at which it is appropriate—or not grossly inappropriate—to adopt a fairly standard policy package. Early monitoring of a

72. The reforms proposed below do not rule out new borrowing, but they do not rely on it heavily. The GAB would stay in place for the foreseeable future to protect the Fund's liquidity, but borrowing under the GAB would take place in SDRs rather than national currencies. Borrowing from private markets might take place too, but mainly to promote the role of the SDR in international capital markets and help to regulate the stock of SDRs held in national reserves.

73. Cooper, "Comment," p. 570.

country's problem can be helpful and cannot be harmful, but an early application of conditionality may be quite harmful, as it is necessarily based on incomplete information. The Fund has drawn this distinction in its guidelines on conditionality, as noted earlier, but should carry it farther. I will propose a method to foster early monitoring and convey to each member the Fund's views about the policies that the member would have to adopt if it sought to use Fund credit at that particular time and thus had to meet the Fund's policy requirements.

If governments must have the right to make their own mistakes and the Fund must have time to make accurate diagnoses, then governments need access to adequate financing before they are ready to use Fund credit and meet the policy conditions attaching to its use. Furthermore, each government deserves some freedom to decide when and how fully to reconstitute its access to financing—when to run a balance of payments surplus and how large it should be. Therefore, I will propose ways of making the Fund emphasize reserve creation rather than focusing primarily on the supply of reserve credit.

It would also be wise to preserve and enlarge the compensatory financing facility and lift the restrictions recently imposed on access to the CFF.[74] The need for the CFF would be reduced if the Fund turned from the provision of reserve credit to the creation of reserves, because governments can use reserves at their discretion. But that is not likely to happen quickly, and it is more efficient in welfare-theoretic terms to finance export shortfalls than to stabilize export prices or receipts by international commodity agreements. By maintaining and enlarging the CFF, the international community can honor in a modest way the principle of compensation for innocent victims without having to assess culpability.

---

74. To draw an amount no larger than 50 percent of its quota, a member must demonstrate its willingness to "cooperate with the Fund" in finding "appropriate solutions" for its balance of payments difficulties. Previously, a member could satisfy that requirement by a serious undertaking to discuss with the Fund the measures that might be required. In 1983, the interpretation was tightened. "Where the Fund considers that the existing policies of the member . . . are seriously deficient or where the country's record of cooperation in the recent past has been unsatisfactory, the Fund will expect the member to take action that gives, prior to submission of the request for the purchase, a reasonable assurance that policies corrective of the member's balance of payments problem will be adopted" (IMF, *Annual Report, 1984,* p. 137). Furthermore, the Fund reduced from 100 to 83 percent of quota the total amount that a member can draw from the CFF, and it tightened terms of access to the upper 33 percent, making them virtually the same as those governing access to the upper credit tranches. "As a result of these changes the CFF has largely become a supplement to general conditional access for those countries that meet not only the general test of the Fund's conditionality but also the criteria for an export shortfall" (Polak, "Role of the Fund," p. 254).

Fund credit is for "temporary use" in dealing with balance of payments deficits, and conditionality is meant in part to guarantee that deficits are temporary. It does not necessarily follow, however, that users of Fund credit should repay it quickly. Once again, the allowable length of time for repayment depends both on the size of the balance of payments surplus that a user of Fund credit can be expected to run after it has ended its deficit and on the speed at which it can generate that surplus. Therefore, the Fund should be able to vary its repayment terms from case to case and time to time. It should be able to make allowance for its members' circumstances and for the state of the world economy. Rapid repayments are appropriate at times of high economic activity and inflationary pressures, when it would be right for many countries to reduce aggregate demand and run balance of payments surpluses; they are less appropriate at times of low activity.[75]

Finally, a strong case can be made for increasing the supply of financing available through the Fund. Its resources should not be used to cover long-lasting current account deficits like those run by many countries in the 1970s. The Fund was not created to engage in continuing intermediation—to facilitate ongoing transfers of real resources from high savers to low savers or from rich to poor. It may indeed be hard pressed to do its traditional task—to finance temporary balance of payments deficits and give countries time to adjust to permanent shocks.

Now that the supply of bank loans has been curtailed sharply, the governments of some less developed countries want the Fund to redefine its role and cover part of the shortfall. By trying to divert it to this purpose, however, they are likely to injure their own interests—to antagonize those governments that want the Fund to discharge its original mandate and that are willing to provide resources only for that purpose. The developing nations have already hurt themselves by their tenacious defense of the case for linking SDR creation with development assistance, because they have

75. Under Article V, sec. 7(c), the Fund can decide by an 85 percent majority to lengthen or shorten the repayment period for all its members. Under sec. 7(g), a member may ask the Fund to lengthen the period applying to that member "because discharge on the due date would result in exceptional hardship for the member," and the Fund can decide to do so by a 70 percent majority. If it used sec. 7(c) to shorten the repayment period for all members, it would have to give adequate warning and be prepared to make exceptions under sec. 7(g). The Fund's ability to vary its repayment terms through time might depend on its own liquidity, and that is one reason for wanting the Fund to be large. Under the arrangements proposed below, moreover, its ability to alter its terms would help it to regulate the volume of reserves, because all of its transactions would be conducted in SDRs. By lengthening repayments of Fund credit, the Fund could raise temporarily the growth rate of SDR holdings.

led other governments to be suspicious of *any* argument for an SDR allocation, so that allocations have been small and intermittent.

Similar considerations argue against blurring traditional distinctions between the Fund and the World Bank. The two institutions should be identifiable clearly, not only with respect to the purposes for which they make credit available and the terms on which they lend, but also with respect to the ways in which they are financed. That is one reason why market borrowing by the Fund does not feature prominently in the proposals that follow. The Fund and Bank must cooperate closely, because they bring different skills to bear on the analysis of a country's problems and because some countries' problems require "structural" adjustment. But financing from the Fund should be made available for rapid use and carefully conditioned primarily on resort to appropriate macroeconomic policies, whereas financing from the Bank should be made available for more gradual use and carefully conditioned on the implementation of microeconomic policies designed to reallocate resources and use them efficiently.[76] Countries should be encouraged to draw on both institutions. In certain cases, moreover, they should be allowed to repay them at the slow rate customarily associated with World Bank loans. But the two institutions should continue to specialize in approving and monitoring different classes of policies.

How large must the Fund be to fulfill its traditional role? No one can claim to know. The answer depends in the first instance on the sizes of disturbances likely to affect both current and capital accounts. But it also depends on the choices that governments make between financing and adjustment, and those choices are not independent of the collective decisions made concerning the aggregate supply of financing and the conditions attaching to its use. Furthermore, the demand for financing does not focus wholly on the Fund. It can be satisfied by using currency reserves and borrowing from official institutions other than the Fund, as well as by borrowing from private institutions.

The total demand for financing from official sources will probably be smaller in the years ahead than in the recent past, even though the supply from banks and other private sources will be smaller and less reliable. Governments are likely to keep their economies under closer control,

76. In light of the recent enthusiasm for an increase in policy-related World Bank lending, it is perhaps appropriate to warn against tarnishing the Bank's "seal of approval" in the way that the Fund's "seal of approval" was tarnished by the need for a rapid response to the debt crisis of 1982–83, when the Fund was obliged to endorse unrealistic policies and Fund conditionality became too closely identified with bankers' notions about creditworthiness.

opting for more adjustment and less financing than in the 1970s. But it would not be wise to expect a steady decline in the demand for financing from official sources. It would be more prudent to expect a one-time drop from the levels observed during the debt crisis, when funding from official sources had to replace funding from private sources, and a gradual increase thereafter, no slower than the growth rate of world trade.

Furthermore, the demand for financing from the Fund may grow faster than the total demand for financing from official sources. Reserves, even those of industrial countries, have been falling relative to trade and some of the heavily indebted countries have drawn theirs down sharply. They cannot allow them to fall farther and should be trying to rebuild them.[77]

Matched against any measure of the potential demand for financing from the Fund, its present resources are not very large. Total quotas were raised to 5.3 percent of world imports in 1983 but that percentage was still below the average in the 1960s, and some of the extra resources provided by the quota increase were used or committed very quickly. There is also the unprecedented possibility that obligations to the Fund itself may have to be rescheduled if countries with severe debt problems cannot solve them soon. In other words, the Fund's resources may not revolve.

Reforming the Fund

The proposals advanced here are limited in scope. They relate to the functioning of the Fund itself, not of the whole monetary system, and they focus primarily on the Fund's role as a financial institution, not as a monitor of exchange rate arrangements. They are designed to deal with problems raised in earlier parts of this paper—the need to improve the administration of conditionality and to give more emphasis to reserve creation. But they will also clarify the rights and obligations that attach to membership in the Fund, especially the obligation to supply financing. And they will serve other long-term objectives by making it easier for governments to use the Fund for consolidating and managing the stock of reserves. These latter objectives will not get much attention here, however, because I have examined them elsewhere.[78]

My proposals focus on the role of the SDR, not with the aim of making it "the principal reserve asset in the international monetary system" (Article VIII, sec. 7), but with the narrower aim of making it the Fund's own

---

77. See John Williamson, *A New SDR Allocation?* (Washington, D.C.: Institute for International Economics, 1984), pp. 20–31.
78. Kenen, "Use of the SDR."

currency and more useful for purposes of reserve creation. They would lead to a Fund based fully on the SDR but not in the way usually associated with that phrase.[79] The General and Special Drawing Rights Departments of the Fund would not be merged, but the boundary between them would be redrawn.

Under present arrangements, the Fund supplies three types of balance of payments financing:

—It allocates new SDRs in proportion to members' quotas, and these function as reserves. They can be transferred freely between members willing to engage in such transfers, but a member wanting to sell them for another member's currency and unable to find a buyer can ask the Fund to designate a buyer, subject to the requirements and restrictions mentioned earlier. Members do not have to reconstitute their holdings of SDRs.

—It credits members with reserve positions equal in value to one quarter of their quotas (the quarter corresponding to the fraction of subscriptions paid in reserve assets), and a member's reserve position grows automatically when the Fund sells its currency to another member. Reserve positions are counted as reserves because members can draw on them freely without meeting policy conditions or repaying their drawings.

—It makes Fund credit available to members in amounts based on their quotas. But credit tranche drawings must be approved by the Fund, and drawings beyond the first credit tranche are subject to explicit policy conditions, which increase in stringency with the size of the drawing. Furthermore, Fund credit must be repaid.

The first form of financing is provided through the SDR Department of the Fund, and decisions about quantities are made on the recommendation of the managing director according to criteria set out explicitly in the Fund agreement (Article XVIII, sec. 1). The second and third forms of financing are provided through the General Department, and decisions about quantities are made at five-year intervals, when Fund quotas are reviewed, but without reference to particular criteria (Article III, sec. 2).

Although there are three ways in which the Fund provides financing, there are only two ways in which its members provide financing through the Fund and thus two limits on their obligations. First, they are required to accept SDRs when designated by the Fund, but only when their holdings of SDRs are not more than three times as large as their cumulative allocations. Second, they place their own currencies at the disposal of the Fund in amounts equal in value to three-fourths of their quotas (an amount

---

79. See, for example, J. J. Polak, *Thoughts on an International Monetary Fund Based Fully on the SDR*, IMF Pamphlet Series 28 (IMF, 1979).

corresponding to the fraction of subscriptions paid in national currencies); these are the currencies used by the General Department to finance reserve tranche and credit tranche drawings.

The acceptance limit applies directly to financing through the SDR Department, but it also affects a member's obligation to provide financing through the General Department, which holds and sells SDRs as well as currencies. The size of a member's quota limits its obligation to provide financing through the General Department, and the limit may be framed in terms of the member's obligation to accept an increase in its own reserve position; it starts at 25 percent of quota and cannot normally rise beyond 100 percent (which limits it to 400 percent of its initial level).

These arrangements are unnecessarily complicated. They blur the basic functional difference between the two departments of the Fund. Both departments are involved in creating reserve assets, because SDR holdings reside in the SDR Department but reserve positions reside in the General Department, and both departments are affected by the limit on a member's obligation to accept SDRs. Furthermore, current arrangements blur the nature of each member's rights and obligations. Its rights are defined with respect to SDR holdings, reserve positions, and access to Fund credit; its obligations are defined by its acceptance limit and its currency subscription. Finally, basic decisions are not integrated. There is no single time for looking at the size of the Fund as a whole in relation to global needs and to supplies of financing from other sources.

The Fund's present structure would appear to give it some flexibility in raising additional resources from its members. Although an increase in Fund quotas requires legislation in many member countries, and must even go through the budgetary process in the United States, an SDR allocation does not face these hurdles. But this distinction has been breaking down in the United States, the country in which it has mattered most. In 1983, when Congress approved the most recent increase in the U.S. quota, it added new language to the Bretton Woods Agreement Act:

Neither the President nor any person or agency shall on behalf of the United States vote to allocate Special Drawing Rights under Article XVIII, Sections 2 and 3, of the Articles of Agreement of the Fund without consultations by the Secretary of the Treasury at least 90 days prior to any such vote, with the Chairman and ranking minority members of the Committee on Foreign Relations and the Committee on Banking, Housing, and Urban Affairs of the Senate and the Committee on Banking, Finance, and Urban Affairs of the House of Representatives, and the appropriate subcommittees thereof.[80]

80. 22 U.S.C. 286q.

Similar language applies to any undertaking by the United States with regard to its obligations under the GAB (and to market borrowing by the Fund if it will be dollar denominated).[81] Furthermore, governments and central banks have begun to look at their positions in the Fund on an integrated basis. The Bundesbank has recently expressed concern about the large size of Germany's claims on the Fund in relation to German reserves.[82]

The Fund's structure should be altered in ways that would consolidate its reserve-creating activities and simplify its members' obligation to provide financing through the Fund. All decisions affecting the size of the Fund should be taken on the basis of consistent criteria relating to the need for balance of payments financing, supplies of reserves and reserve credit from other sources, and the appropriate division of Fund-related financing between reserve creation and the provision of reserve credit.

Decisions about the division of financing should seek to balance the two sets of criteria stressed in this paper. By exercising influence on the supply of reserves, the Fund can affect the amount of autonomy that governments enjoy in framing their balance of payments policies. Facing uncertainty about the nature and duration of a payments deficit, a government may want to finance it rather than adjust immediately, or to combine financing with adjustment. Thereafter, it will want to decide how fully and rapidly to reconstitute its access to financing. By exercising influence on the supply of reserve credit, the Fund can affect its own ability to influence national policies and thus represent the collective interests of its members. Governments will have reason to heed its advice if it has large amounts of credit at its disposal.

These objectives can be advanced by shifting the boundary between the two departments of the Fund and altering the manner in which the Fund applies conditionality.

81. The language relating to the GAB is much stricter; the U.S. executive director cannot consent to any increase in the amount, terms, or conditions of U.S. participation without congressional authorization.

82. Cited in Polak, "Role of the Fund," p. 264. According to Polak's own calculations, Germany's actual claims on the Fund totaled 13 percent of its nongold reserves at the end of 1983, but its potential claims amounted to 28 percent. (He defines potential claims in a way that makes them measure a country's total obligation to provide financing through the Fund. They equal 300 percent of its SDR allocation, which measures the first obligation listed above, plus its total quota, which measures the second obligation, plus its whole commitment under the GAB.) Polak points out that Germany's potential claims are smaller than those of other major countries, which range from 38 percent for Japan and 50 percent for France to 126 percent for the United Kingdom and 170 percent for the United States.

Although the value of the SDR is now defined by a composite of five national currencies (francs, marks, yens, pounds, and dollars), it is not "backed" by anything. It is an "outside" asset, pure and simple. The SDR Department of the Fund does not hold any assets; it has only notional claims on Fund members equal to their cumulative allocations (which are used to calculate interest charges and acceptance limits). Similarly, a member does not incur any debt to the Fund when SDRs are allocated to it; its only obligation is the peculiar requirement that it accept *more* SDRs in exchange for its own currency if it is designated by the Fund.

These are attractive characteristics from some points of view, because they distinguish SDRs from most other reserve assets. The stock of SDRs cannot implode on account of a shift in governments' portfolio preferences; no one can ask the Fund to redeem them in currencies, gold, or anything else. But those same characteristics make it hard for many intelligent people to understand the SDR, including people who have to make decisions about it. They may indeed exacerbate concerns about the "inflationary consequences" of creating SDRs. It might be better to make SDRs more "conventional" by changing the way that they are issued without also changing their most important attribute—that holders cannot cash them in for other reserve assets. The SDR Department might sell new SDRs for national currencies without standing ready to buy them back. The currencies would be held by the SDR Department, in lieu of notional claims on Fund members.

To start this reorganization, the SDR Department would sell SDRs to each member of the Fund in exchange for the member's own currency, in an amount sufficient for the member to buy back its currency subscription from the General Department.[83] The SDR Department would hold the

---

83. This process would take time, because the currency holdings of the General Department do not equal the subscriptions of the issuing countries. If a member has drawn on the Fund and has not repurchased its currency, the Fund's holdings will be larger than the member's subscription. If a member's currency has been used in drawings, the Fund's holdings will be smaller than the member's subscription. Eventually, however, members could buy back "excess" holdings of their own currencies, using the currencies of other members, and the unscrambling of assets could be completed. (I have not tied down two loose ends—the disposition of the gold held by the General Department and the "backing" of the SDRs already issued by the SDR Department. There are many ways of dealing with the gold; it could be left where it is, repurchased along with national currencies and turned over to the SDR Department, repurchased and retained by members, or auctioned off in the free market. There are two ways of dealing with SDRs already issued. They could be treated as a fixed fiduciary issue against which the SDR Department would not hold national

currencies as "backing" for the stock of SDRs (and the maintenance-of-value obligation in Article V, sec. 11, of the Fund agreement would apply to those currencies, instead of currencies held by the General Department). The General Department would hold SDRs, rather than national currencies, and use them in all of its subsequent transactions.

Thereafter, the SDR Department would sell SDRs to members whenever the Fund decided to enlarge the supply of Fund credit available from the General Department by increasing quotas, to enlarge the supply of Fund-related reserve assets by increasing members' SDR holdings directly, or to consolidate reserve assets by substituting SDRs for currency or gold reserves. In the first two cases, SDRs would be sold to members in exchange for their own currencies. In the first, they would be sold to each member in an amount equal to the increase in its quota (unless a member chose to pay for the increase with SDRs it was already holding and thus opted out of the allocation). In the second case, new SDRs would be sold to each member in proportion to its quota, as under present arrangements.[84] In the third case, involving the substitution of SDRs for other reserve assets, new SDRs would be sold to members in exchange for other members' currencies (dollars, for example), but only with the explicit consent of the members issuing those currencies and in amounts agreeable to them.[85]

---

currencies; that would perpetuate the present arrangement in respect of those SDRs. Alternatively, members could "purchase" them retroactively by depositing national currencies with the SDR Department. I assume retroactive repurchases below, when discussing the recalculation of acceptance limits.)

84. It might be useful, however, to impart more flexibility to those arrangements by authorizing the SDR Department to sell SDRs to some groups of countries, such as those with small quotas, without selling them to others (or to sell more to some than to others, relative to quotas). Departures from uniformity could take place when approved by large majorities. In any case, decisions to allocate SDRs must give more weight to the interests of small countries; although they make up most of the Fund's membership, its decisions have been dominated by the views and interests of large countries. The notion of "global need" should take into account the needs of the majority of members, not concentrate on those of a few large countries, although they hold most of the world's reserves and will necessarily receive much of any allocation. Polak makes a similar point: "SDR creation favors the reserve needs of weaker countries; but the fact that the stronger members of the Fund, and in particular the reserve centers, can get by comfortably without this credit mechanism of the Fund is not a good reason not to allow it to perform the useful international function that it can perform" ("Role of the Fund," p. 260).

85. This scheme for substitution is consistent with one I outlined in an earlier paper ("Use of the SDR," pp. 352–55). Under that earlier plan, substitution would be voluntary but limited in timing and amount. Members of the Fund might agree, for example, to open up the option for a five-year period but limit its use by any single member; the limit could be tied to the member's gross reserves or Fund quota but would not have to be completely uniform. Under that plan, however, reserve currencies sold to the Fund were to be segre-

The SDR Department would earn interest on its currency holdings, and would be paid in SDRs. The applicable interest rate would be the same as that paid by the Fund on actual holdings of SDRs, including those of the General Department. Therefore, interest-income flows would be self-balancing, much as they are now. The national currencies would also be used to calculate acceptance limits. Those limits would have to rise sharply in absolute terms, because they would replace two limits that operate additively now, but could be somewhat lower in percentage terms than they are currently.

At present, a member may be required to accept SDRs until its total holdings reach 300 percent of its cumulative allocation. But it also supplies credit through the General Department, where its obligation is defined by its currency subscription. The new acceptance limits would have to be large enough to replace the sum of these two obligations, but this could be done by setting them at 250 percent of the member's currency balance held by the SDR Department.

Consider the case of the United States. Its quota in the Fund is SDR 17.9 billion, and its currency subscription is thus SDR 13.4 billion. Its cumulative SDR allocation is SDR 4.9 billion, which means that it can be required to accept an additional SDR 9.8 billion under current rules.[86] Accordingly, its total obligation to provide financing through the Fund amounts to SDR 23.2 billion (apart from its obligation under the GAB).

---

gated from other assets (and several suggestions were made regarding their subsequent use); under the present proposal, the currencies would lie dormant in the SDR Department, along with all other currencies purchased in exchange for new SDRs. As all such currencies would be subject to a maintenance-of-value requirement and would be used to calculate acceptance limits, substitution through the SDR Department would impose new obligations on the countries issuing the reserve currencies—the United States in particular. Furthermore, those countries would have to pay interest on holdings by the SDR Department, and this could cause problems if, as proposed below, they had to pay in SDRs. In another paper, I showed that U.S. holdings of SDRs might be too small for this purpose; see Peter B. Kenen, "The Analytics of a Substitution Account," *Banca Nazionale del Lavoro Quarterly Review,* vol. 34 (December 1981), pp. 403–26. The problem could be solved, however, if the United States could make dollar interest payments in respect of dollars transferred to the SDR Department via substitution. The SDR Department would keep the dollar payments and issue extra SDRs against them. In effect, it would engage in supplementary substitution.

86. Polak points out that the unused acceptance obligation of the United States has been large enough most of the time to absorb the holdings of all other industrial countries (Polak, "Role of the Fund," p. 265). On June 30, 1985, the actual holdings of the United States were SDR 1.3 billion larger than its cumulative allocation, so that its unused acceptance limit was SDR 8.5 billion. On that same date, the actual holdings of other industrial countries totaled only SDR 8.1 billion. (Those of *all* other countries came to SDR 11.0 billion, so that the United States could have absorbed all but SDR 2.5 billion of the total stock held by governments, but the General Department of the Fund held an additional SDR 4.2 billion.)

Under the plan proposed here, its currency subscription would be shifted to the SDR Department, and it would make an additional dollar payment of SDR 4.9 billion (its retroactive payment for SDRs allocated in the past). Therefore, the SDR Department would hold U.S. dollars worth SDR 18.3 billion. If the new acceptance limit was set at 250 percent of currency holdings in the SDR Department, it would amount to SDR 45.8 billion, and the United States would be required to supply SDR 27.5 billion in financing through the Fund, an amount slightly larger than at present.

Some might say that these arrangements are retrogressive, because SDRs would be backed by and purchased with currencies. But most forms of money must be purchased; central banks create them by buying domestic and foreign securities. Some might say that these arrangements could cripple the Fund, because national legislatures, notably the U.S. Congress, would acquire more influence over its operations. Congress, for example, would control participation by the United States in SDR allocations, whether they were made to raise U.S. holdings or augment the resources of the General Department. Its approval would be needed whenever the United States had to use dollars to purchase SDRs. But matters have already moved in this direction, and the introduction of the new arrangements might furnish an occasion—and an argument—for altering the role of Congress vis-à-vis the Fund.

When asked to revise the Bretton Woods Agreement Act to align it with the new structure of the Fund, Congress should be asked to return to an earlier practice. Transactions with the Fund should be treated as exchanges of assets rather than budgetary matters, and the Treasury should be authorized to undertake them whenever they are mandated by Fund decisions. Congressional consent should still be required for any change in the U.S. quota, because quotas would continue to govern voting in the Fund. But Congress should not have to approve the financial transactions required for this and other purposes. The new arrangements, moreover, would make it very sensible for Congress to treat these financial transactions as exchanges of assets; the United States would swap dollars for SDRs whenever there was an increase in Fund quotas, instead of receiving a notional claim on the Fund. (When SDRs were transferred to the General Department, the United States would still obtain a notional claim, but Congress would have to approve those transfers in principle, because it would have to approve any increase in the U.S. quota.)

The General Department and Conditionality

Under the new arrangements, the General Department of the Fund would continue to function as a credit union. It would not become a bank,

68

even though its transactions would take place entirely in SDRs. The total resources of the General Department would be predetermined by the sum of members' quotas, and each member's access to them would be defined by its own quota. But the General Department would be concerned exclusively with the administration of Fund credit. There would be no reserve positions.[87] The General Department would provide reserve credit for use at the discretion of the membership collectively. The SDR Department would provide reserves for use at the discretion of each member individually. Members would provide financing through the two departments jointly, by acquiring SDRs from other members.

This change in structure, however, should be accompanied by a change in the method of administering conditionality. The Fund should apply systematically a notion advanced in its own guidelines.

At an early stage in the development of a country's balance of payments problem, its government may want to draw down reserves rather than use Fund credit. It may be too soon to diagnose accurately the nature and probable duration of its payments problem and too costly to submit to conditionality or the obligation to repay Fund credit. To make an intelligent choice, however, the government must know what conditions it would face if it turned to the Fund at that early stage or later. Therefore, the Fund should administer "shadow" conditionality vis-à-vis all members that appear to be potential users of Fund credit.

Under Article IV, sec. 3(b), of the Fund agreement, the Fund engages in an annual consultation with each member. These consultations afford the Fund an opportunity to "exercise firm surveillance over the exchange rate policies of members," but they range widely over current problems and policies.[88] In the course of these confidential consultations, and more frequently when necessary, the staff of the Fund should make known its views about the member's balance of payments situation and the policy

87. By implication, a member's right to draw on the General Department would not depend on the drawings of other members. A French drawing of yen would not affect Japan's position in the Fund. This mechanism would be replaced by changes in members' holdings of SDRs. If France draws SDRs from the Fund and sells them to Japan for yen, Japan's holdings of SDRs rise, making it possible for Japan to finance a larger balance of payments deficit in the future. (It should perhaps be noted that changes in Fund quotas do not affect reserves under present arrangements and would not affect them under the new arrangements. At present, reserve positions rise with an increase in quotas, but members must pay over SDRs or other reserve assets to enlarge their reserve positions. In the future, an SDR allocation would accompany an increase in quotas, but the new SDRs would be transferred to the General Department for use in extending Fund credit.)

88. Recently, the Fund has begun to engage in multilateral consultations with the five countries whose currencies jointly define the value of the SDR (France, Germany, Japan, the United Kingdom, and the United States). It is too early to judge their effectiveness, however, and they play no role in this discussion.

changes, if any, that would be required to correct it. Its views should be offered to surplus countries as well as deficit countries.

But something more should be done. When the staff of the Fund believes that a member is facing a serious problem, the staff should solicit a "provisional" letter of intent, describing the policies that the member proposes to follow in order to deal with its surplus or deficit. This should not be done routinely; the preparation of a letter of intent is a massive task that involves the most senior policymakers. If requests are made routinely, responses will be made routinely, and they will lose significance. Furthermore, this letter may be more difficult to draft than the one submitted when a member makes a drawing; it must be contingent as well as provisional. It should describe the policies that the member plans to follow, given its current views about its balance of payments problem, and those that it would follow if its surplus or deficit proved to be more obdurate than currently expected. Those that the member plans to follow in light of its current views should be taken to reflect the policy commitments that it would make formally if it applied for a drawing immediately; those that it would follow if forced to revise its views should be taken to reflect the commitments it would make if it applied for a drawing later.

If the staff of the Fund does not object to these plans, the member should have the right to expect that the staff would recommend approval if the plans were embodied in a formal letter of intent submitted in conjunction with a request for a drawing. If the staff believes that a member's plans will not deal adequately with its problem, it should request revision of the provisional letter of intent.

A provisional letter of intent should be appended to the report that the staff submits to the executive board of the Fund, summarizing the results of its consultation. If the staff is not satisfied with the letter, even after it has been revised, the staff should give its reasons to the board, and the board may then choose to pursue the matter. The presumption in favor of doing so should be particularly strong when a surplus or deficit has lasted for some time, resulting in a large one-way movement of reserves (or a large increase in the debt of a deficit country) that could cause future problems. The presumption is also strong when the country involved is large, because the situations of large countries have important implications for the ability of other countries to manage their balance of payments problems and for the integrity of the monetary system.

If the executive board concludes that a member's plans are inadequate, it may decide to make representations to the member, either formally, in its own name, or informally, through the managing director and staff. In the case of a member thought likely to draw on the Fund, the executive board should indicate its dissatisfaction explicitly and give its reasons, so that the member will know that it cannot expect to draw on the Fund unless it changes its plans.

Proposals of this sort have been made before. It is time to implement them, even without putting in place the long-run structural reforms suggested earlier. The introduction of shadow conditionality would contribute in three ways to the effectiveness of Fund surveillance and administration of conditionality. First, it would give sharper focus to the annual consultations and induce senior policymakers to participate more frequently, rather than involve themselves with the Fund only on the eve of a drawing. Second, it would reduce the time and effort needed to negotiate a standby arrangement once a member had decided to request one, because the views of the Fund and the member would be known to each other, and the member would be spared unpleasant surprises. Finally, a member could start to make policy changes before turning to the Fund, knowing what the Fund is likely to require. It would not have to make them abruptly and thus concede conspicuously that it has bowed to the judgment of the Fund.

The Fund and Private Markets

In 1982–83, when there was much concern about the Fund's liquidity, it was suggested that Fund supplement its resources by borrowing from international capital markets.[89] Enthusiasm has died down, however, because the Fund has replenished its resources by increasing quotas and because many members want to reduce the Fund's reliance on borrowed resources.

Borrowing from private markets did not feature in the proposals made above, partly because it seems wise to preserve the principle of mutuality, which calls on governments to furnish the resources needed by the Fund. But there are additional arguments against it. Recent events suggest that governments should not rely on private markets for balance of payments financing. They can be fair-weather friends. The Fund should not rely on them either, although markets are less likely to freeze up on the Fund than on individual countries. Furthermore, the Fund and World Bank should strive to be different, not only in the purposes for which they provide financing but also in the ways in which they finance themselves. The Bank is well established in international capital markets and will have to use

---

89. The idea began to receive attention earlier, when Saudi Arabia gave strong backing to observer status for the Palestine Liberation Organization, and it was feared that Saudi Arabia might refuse to lend more to the Fund if its views did not prevail.

them heavily if it is to fill part of the gap left by the reduction in bank lending to developing countries. The Fund should not compete with it.

Yet there may be a role for market borrowing in making the SDR a more attractive reserve asset, and that effort will acquire new importance under the proposals made in this paper. The willingness of members to hold SDRs will determine the ability of the Fund to create reserves and furnish reserve credit.

For some time to come, the transferability of the SDR will depend on the designation procedure. For that same reason, however, it will be restricted by acceptance limits. The two devices go together, because governments will not expose themselves to designation unless they are protected by acceptance limits. In the long run, however, the transferability of the SDR and thus the Fund's own access to financing should be underwritten by its members' appetite for SDRs—a development that would gradually lead the Fund to function as a bank rather than a credit union.

Much has been done to make the SDR more attractive and thus increase the willingness of governments to hold it. But most of the measures have concentrated on its role as a store of value. The currency basket defining its value has been simplified; its interest rate has been redefined and brought more closely into line with market interest rates; restrictions on its use have been eliminated; and the reconstitution requirement has been abolished.[90] Little has been done to make the SDR a useful means of payment—an asset that governments can buy and sell on foreign exchange markets. When governments use reserves to finance balance of payments deficits, they do not transfer them directly to other governments. Instead, they intervene on foreign exchange markets and transfer reserve assets to private institutions. To make the SDR more attractive as a reserve asset, it

---

90. Williamson has recently suggested that the reconstitution rule be reintroduced to pave the way politically for a large SDR allocation: "With a reintroduction of the reconstitution provision, the objection that 'loans' as a result of SDR allocation would be of indefinite duration would lose much of its own force. The principle would be reestablished that the SDR system is intended to provide reserves-to-hold, not to transfer real resources" (Williamson, *A New SDR Allocation?* p. 40). Williamson may be right about the politics; reintroduction of the requirement might allay the fears of governments that do not want to transfer more resources to others—to those that would spend new SDRs rather than retain them. As a practical matter, however, reconstitution would not be an adequate barrier to spending unless the requirement was made more onerous than the one adopted in 1969. Furthermore, its reintroduction would make the SDR more like a form of credit and less like a reserve asset, and this paper has argued that the Fund must pay more attention to reserve creation.

should be made more usable as a means of payment and, therefore, transferable to private institutions.[91]

Transferability could be achieved by permitting private institutions to hold SDRs on the books of the Fund, but this would be cumbersome. It would add hugely to the volume of transactions crossing the Fund's books. It would also complicate decisions in the Fund, because decisions affecting the supply of officially issued SDRs would be seen to affect private sector liquidity and thus to impinge on the responsibilities of national monetary authorities. Transferability can be achieved, however, by setting up a clearinghouse for private transactions in SDRs and using it to link official SDRs on the books of the Fund with private SDRs on the books of private institutions.

Transactions between commercial banks involving private SDRs would take place on the books of the clearinghouse; they would not lead to transfers of official SDRs on the Fund's own books. Transactions between central banks and commercial banks would likewise take place through the clearinghouse, but these would lead to transfers of official SDRs on the books of the SDR Department. Whenever a central bank bought SDRs in the foreign exchange market or borrowed them on the capital market, the clearinghouse would experience a reduction in its liabilities to commercial banks, matched by a reduction in its holdings of official SDRs. The official SDRs would be transferred to the central bank that made the purchase in the market. Borrowing by the Fund itself would likewise lead to a transfer of official SDRs; the holdings of the clearinghouse would fall and those of the General Department would rise.

Creation of a clearinghouse would serve several purposes. It would lead quickly to the standardization of private SDRs and of all assets denominated in them; these differ today in small but important ways, and standardization must occur before SDRs can be used in foreign exchange trading. Once they are used for this purpose, moreover, they can be used for intervention. Furthermore, creation of a clearinghouse would allow official institutions, including the General Department of the Fund, to

---

91. This assertion and the analysis that follows are developed more fully in Kenen, "Use of the SDR," pp. 342–49. The proposal for a clearinghouse made below is likewise detailed there; see also the "Comments" by Richard N. Cooper and John Williamson (pp. 361–62 and 370–73). A similar proposal was made by Warren L. Coats, Jr., "The SDR as a Means of Payment," *International Monetary Fund Staff Papers*, vol. 29 (September 1982), pp. 422–36; see also the exchange involving Coats, myself, Pierre R. van den Boogaerde, and Philippe Callier, in "The SDR as a Means of Payment: A Comment on Coats," *International Monetary Fund Staff Papers*, vol. 30 (September 1983), pp. 650–69.

borrow SDRs from the private sector. At present, they can issue SDR-denominated instruments but cannot add the proceeds to their SDR holdings. Finally, the General Department of the Fund could borrow SDRs not only to supplement its resources but also to reduce official holdings temporarily and thus exercise closer control over the supply of Fund-related reserve assets.[92]

Conclusion

This study has covered many issues. It has traced the evolution of the Fund as a financial institution. It has reviewed the case for financing balance of payments deficits, with particular attention to the comparative merits of using reserves and reserve credit. It has examined the arguments for conditionality and fixed-term repayment, and found good reasons for the former but not for the latter. It has made proposals for long-term reform of the Fund to clarify and simplify its members' rights and obligations and place greater emphasis on its role as a reserve-creating institution. It has proposed a change in the way that the Fund administers conditionality.

The Articles of Agreement of the Fund would have to be amended to implement the proposals for long-term reform. But some of the other recommendations could be implemented right away: the creation of a clearinghouse to give the SDR a wider role in private markets and link private SDRs with official SDRs, the introduction of "shadow" conditionality, and the relaxation of fixed-term repayment. Furthermore, the Fund could pay more attention to reserve creation without any change in organization. As a matter of fact, it could and should start soon to allocate more SDRs.

92. If the General Department of the Fund borrowed SDRs from private holders, the SDR Department would transfer official SDRs from the account of the clearinghouse to the account of the General Department. If the clearinghouse had to replenish its holdings, it would have to ask commercial banks to increase their deposits with it, and they would have to buy more SDRs from their central banks, reducing the holdings of the latter.

Financing and Adjustment by a Small Economy

THIS APPENDIX examines differences between reserve use and reserve-credit use by a small open economy.

The Economy

The economy produces a single good; output at time t is Q_t, labor input is L_t, the home currency price is q_t, and the nominal wage is w_t. Output is subject to shocks, Q_t^s, so

(1) $$Q_t = Q(L_t) + Q_t^s, \qquad Q_L > 0, \qquad Q_{LL} < 0,$$

(2) $$w_t = q_t Q_L(L_t),$$

for $t = 0, 1, 2$. The goods market always clears:

(3) $$Q_t = c_t + c_t^f,$$

where c_t is consumed at home and c_t^f exported.

Households consume a foreign good too; the quantity is m_t, the foreign currency price is 1, and the home currency price is thus equal to the nominal exchange rate, e_t, measured in units of home currency per unit of foreign currency. Households maximize

(4) $$U_t = \sum_t \left(\frac{1}{1+r}\right)^t E_t (c_t^{1-\gamma} m_t^\gamma)^b, \qquad 0 < b < 1,$$

subject to the constraint that

$$q_t c_t + e_t m_t = A_t,$$

where r is the subjective discount rate, A_t is household expenditure (absorption), defined below, and E_t is the expectations operator ($E_t = 1$ with perfect certainty). From the first-order conditions,

75

(5) $$c_t = (1-\gamma)(A_t/q_t), \qquad m_t = \gamma(A_t/e_t),$$

so that

(4a) $$U_t = u\sum_t\left(\frac{1}{1+r}\right)^t\left(\frac{1}{b}\right)E_t a_t^b, \qquad u = b[\gamma^\gamma(1-\gamma)^{1-\gamma}]^b.$$

Here, a_t is real expenditure:

(6) $$a_t = (A_t/p_t), \qquad p_t = q_t^{1-\gamma}e_t^\gamma = q_t z_t^\gamma,$$

where z_t is the real exchange rate:

(7) $$z_t = (e_t/q_t).$$

Therefore, equations 5 can be rewritten as

(5a) $$c_t = (1-\gamma)a_t z_t^\gamma, \qquad m_t = \gamma a_t z_t^{-(1-\gamma)}.$$

Foreign households have the same utility functions as domestic households, so

(8) $$c_t^f = (1-\gamma)a_t^f z_t^\gamma, \qquad a_t^f = (A_t^f/p_t^f),$$

where A_t^f is foreign expenditure measured in foreign currency and p_t^f is the foreign currency price index, which has the same weights as p_t. By implication, $p_t = e_t p_t^f$, so that purchasing power parity always obtains in respect of the price indexes.[93]

The income real wage is

(9) $$y_t = (w_t/p_t) = z_t^{-\gamma}(w_t/q_t) = z_t^{-\gamma}Q_L(L_t).$$

Differentiating and solving for the change in employment,

(10) $$dL_t = -\left(\frac{1}{n}\right)\left[\left(\frac{dy_t}{y_t}\right) + \gamma\left(\frac{dz_t}{z_t}\right)\right], \qquad n = -(Q_{LL}/Q_L) > 0,$$

93. Home and foreign monetary policies that stabilize those indexes will therefore stabilize the nominal exchange rate, even when the real rate is changing. But policies that stabilize output prices will not stabilize the nominal rate, which must change whenever the real rate changes. (It follows that balance of payments financing does not necessarily involve exchange market intervention to stabilize the nominal exchange rate. It does stabilize the real rate, partially or fully.)

which can be used to obtain the change in the income real wage that would keep employment constant:

(11)
$$\left(\frac{dy_t^*}{y_t}\right) = -\gamma\left(\frac{dz_t}{z_t}\right).$$

But the income real wage is sticky in this sense:

(12) $\left(\frac{dy_k}{y_k}\right) = \lambda\left(\frac{dy_k^*}{y_k}\right), \quad \left(\frac{dy_{k+j}}{y_{k+j}}\right) = \left(\frac{dy_{k+j}^*}{y_{k+j}}\right), \quad 0 < \lambda < 1,$

where k is the first period in which an exogenous shock affects employment (so that $j = 1, 2$ when $k = 0$, and $j = 1$ when $k = 1$).

Use overbars to represent initial values (those before $t = 0$) and set $\bar{q} = \bar{e} = 1$ (so that $\bar{p} = \bar{z} = 1$). Use the operator δ to denote differences between current and initial values measured by linear approximations. From equations 10 and 12,

(10a)
$$\delta L_k = -\left(\frac{1}{n}\right)\gamma(1 - \lambda)\delta z_k, \qquad \delta L_{k+j} = 0.$$

When a disturbance alters the real exchange rate, the contemporaneous change in the income real wage is too small to prevent a change in employment. But wage adjustment is completed one period later, even if the real exchange rate goes on changing, and employment returns to its initial level.[94] Differentiating equation 1 and using equations 10a,

(13)
$$\delta Q_k = -Q_L\left(\frac{1}{n}\right)\gamma(1 - \lambda)\delta z_k + Q_k^\xi, \qquad \delta Q_{k+j} = \sigma_j Q_k^\xi,$$

where σ_j is the fraction of any shock at $t = k$ that survives until $t = k+j$. (If the shock is temporary, $\sigma_j = 0$ for all j; if it is permanent, $\sigma_j = 1$ for all j.)

To obtain the change in the real exchange rate, substitute equations 5a and 8 into equation 3 and differentiate:

94. This formulation is defective in two important ways. There will be partial adjustment in y_k and, therefore, a change in L_k even when $z_{k+1} = \bar{z}$ (when the change in the real exchange rate is transitory). But there will be no adjustment in y_{k-1} when $z_{k-1} \neq \bar{z}$, which happens when the government is able to forecast a disturbance at $t = k$ and to take anticipatory action. (For this second reason, we will not examine employment effects of policy responses to anticipated shocks.)

(14)
$$dQ_t = \gamma Q_t \left(\frac{dz_t}{z_t} \right) + \left(\frac{c_t}{a_t} \right) da_t - C_t^s,$$

where C_t^s is an exogenous reduction in foreign demand:

$$C_t^s = -(1 - \gamma) z_t^{\gamma} da_t^f.$$

But $\bar{c} = (1 - \gamma)\bar{a}$, so

(14a)
$$\delta Q_k = (\gamma \bar{Q}) \delta z_k + (1 - \gamma) \delta a_k - C_k^s,$$

$$\delta Q_{k+j} = (\gamma \bar{Q}) \delta z_{k+j} + (1 - \gamma) \delta a_{k+j} - \sigma_j C_k^s.$$

Combining equations 13 and 14a and solving for the change in the real exchange rate,

$$\delta z_k = \left(\frac{n}{\gamma} \right) \theta [Q_k^s + C_k^s - (1 - \gamma) \delta a_k], \qquad \theta = [n\bar{Q} + (1 - \lambda) Q_L]^{-1},$$

(15)
$$\delta z_{k+j} = \left(\frac{1}{\gamma \bar{Q}} \right) [\sigma_j (Q_k^s + C_k^s) - (1 - \gamma) \delta a_{k+j}].$$

Households do not borrow or lend. The government does it for them. Therefore,

(16)
$$A_t = q_t Q_t - T_t,$$

where T_t is a lump-sum tax (transfer when negative). The government does not produce or consume. It merely regulates real expenditure by taxing, borrowing, and lending. Its foreign currency debt is F_t at the end of period t, and this is its budget constraint:

(17)
$$T_t + e_t F_t - e_t (1 + i) F_{t-1} = 0,$$

where i is the (constant) interest rate paid on foreign currency debt and earned on foreign currency claims. In what follows, $F_{t-1} = 0$ at $t = 0$, so that $\bar{F} = 0$, and $F_t = 0$ at $t = 2$.[95]

95. When F_t is interpreted as reserve use, the restriction $\bar{F} = 0$ can be taken to say that the country begins with a stock of special drawing rights equal to its cumulative allocation, so that it does not earn or pay interest on its reserves. On this same interpretation, the restriction $F_t = 0$ at $t = 2$ must be taken to say that the country reconstitutes reserves completely. This is unrealistically strict, but it makes for close comparability between

Solving equation 17 for T_t, substituting into equation 16 and dividing through by p_t,

$$(18) \qquad a_t = z_t^{-\gamma}[Q_t + f_t - (1 + i)(1 + \pi_t)f_{t-1}],$$

where $f_t = z_t F_t$ and $\pi_t = (z_t - z_{t-1})/z_{t-1}$, and where $f_{t-1} = 0$ at $t = 0$ and $f_t = 0$ at $t = 2$.

Two interpretations can be attached to the f_t. First, they can be deemed to reflect the use of fixed-term reserve credit. In this case, the government can borrow only when it has a contemporaneous balance of payments need, a circumstance represented here by $C_k^s > 0$, and it must repay one period later. Formally, $f_k > 0$ only if $C_k^s > 0$, and $f_t = 0$ for $t \neq k$. Second, they can be deemed to reflect the use of owned reserves. In this case, there are no restrictions on the f_t other than those imposed above, and net use occurs in period $t + 1$ when $f_{t+1} > (1 + \pi_{t+1})f_t$. When making plans at t, however, the government will be assumed to set $\pi_{t+1} = 0$. Therefore, it can be said to plan net use at $t+1$ whenever $f_{t+1}^* > f_t$, where f_{t+1}^* is the value of f_{t+1} planned at t.

Returning to equation 18, define

$$(19) \qquad \delta a_t = \delta Q_t + f_t - (1 + i)(1 + \pi_t)f_{t-1} - (\gamma \bar{Q})\delta z_t,$$

which can be combined with equation 14a to define the government's expectation about the path of real expenditure.

(A) When disturbances originate at $t = 0$ (so $k = 0$), the government knows a_0 but must forecast a_1 and a_2:

$$\delta a_0 = \left(\frac{1}{\gamma}\right)(f_0 - C_0^s),$$

$$(19a) \qquad \delta a_1^* = \left(\frac{1}{\gamma}\right)[f^* - (1 + i)(1 + \pi_1^*)f_0 - \sigma_1^* C_0^s],$$

$$\delta a_2^* = -\left(\frac{1}{\gamma}\right)[(1 + i)(1 + \pi_2^*)f_1^* + \sigma_2^* C_0^s],$$

where asterisks denote anticipated or planned values. Note that the output shocks, Q_k^s, do not figure in these equations or in those below. This is an artifact of the Cobb-Douglas specification embodied in equation 4.

---

reserve use and reserve-credit use; reserve use does not have interest-income effects in periods following $t = 2$.

(B) When disturbances originate at $t = 1$ (so $k = 1$) but are foreseen at $t = 0$, the government knows a_0, as before, but has again to forecast a_1 and a_2:

$$\delta a_0 = \left(\frac{1}{\gamma}\right) f_0,$$

(19b)
$$\delta a_1^* = \left(\frac{1}{\gamma}\right)[f_1^* - (1 + i)(1 + \pi_1^*)f_0 - C_1^{s*}],$$

$$\delta a_2^* = -\left(\frac{1}{\gamma}\right)[(1 + i)(1 + \pi_2^*)f_1^* + \sigma_2^* C_1^{s*}].$$

(C) When disturbances originate at $t = 1$ but are not foreseen at $t = 0$, the government cannot take anticipatory action ($f_0 = 0$). Furthermore, it knows a_1 and has only to forecast a_2:

$$\delta a_0 = 0,$$

(19c)
$$\delta a_1 = \left(\frac{1}{\gamma}\right)(f_1 - C_1^s),$$

$$\delta a_2^* = -\left(\frac{1}{\gamma}\right)[(1 + i)(1 + \pi_2^*)f_1 + \sigma_2^* C_1^s].$$

In every case considered below, however, the government makes its plans on the assumption that $\pi_t^* = 0.$[96]

Maximizing Household Welfare

Suppose that the government is concerned exclusively to maximize its households' welfare. It chooses those f_t that maximize U_t, defined by equation 4a, which is what households would do on their own if they could borrow and lend freely at the interest rate i. The first three cases consid-

---

96. This simplification is imposed not only to simplify equations 19a through 19c but also to simplify the derivatives of equation 18, which are used in the optimizations that follow. It is a strong simplification. When $\pi_t^* > 0$, there will be less balance of payments financing at $t - 1$ than the amount shown as optimal in the examples that follow. Furthermore, there will be financing when none occurs in those examples: (1) with temporary and permanent output shocks, which do not lead to financing in any example below because they do not appear in equations 19a through 19c; and (2) with permanent reductions in foreign demand, which alter z_k differently than z_{k+j} when there is wage stickiness.

ered here ignore uncertainty; the government acts as though it knows the values of C_k^*, σ_1^*, and σ_2^*. The fourth case allows for uncertainty about the values of σ_1^* and σ_2^* (about the permanence of the disturbances).

In the first and simplest case, the disturbance occurs at $t = 1$ and is unanticipated. Therefore, $f_0 = 0$, and the government has merely to choose the value of f_1 that maximizes U_t. The first-order condition is

$$(20) \qquad \left(\frac{1}{1+r}\right)a_1^{b-1}\left(\frac{\partial a_1}{\partial f_1}\right) + \left[\left(\frac{1}{1+r}\right)^2\right]a_2^{*b-1}\left(\frac{\partial a_2^*}{\partial f_1}\right) = 0,$$

and from equation 18,

$$(21) \qquad \left(\frac{\partial a_2}{\partial f_1}\right) = -(1+i)(1+\pi_2^*)^{1-\gamma}\left(\frac{\partial a_1^*}{\partial f_1}\right).$$

But $\pi_2^* = 0$, by assumption, so that

$$(20a) \qquad a_1^{b-1} = \left(\frac{1+i}{1+r}\right)a_2^{*b-1}.$$

Here and hereafter, however, the interest rate equals the discount rate ($i = r$), so that $a_1 = a_2^*$, and from equations 19c,

$$(22) \qquad f_1 = \left(\frac{1}{2+i}\right)(1 - \sigma_2^*)C_1^s.$$

If the reduction in foreign demand is seen to be temporary ($\sigma_2^* = 0$), then $f_1 \approx (1/2)C_1^s$. There is partial financing, and it raises household welfare compared to the level that would obtain with $f_1 = 0$.[97] If the reduction in

97. There are two ways to prove this statement. First, as the value of f_1 given by equation 22 is the one that maximizes U_t for the disturbance C_1^s, it must yield a value for U_t higher than the value that would obtain if f_1 were constrained to zero. Second, differentiating equation 4a,

$$dU_t = u\Sigma_t\left(\frac{1}{1+r}\right)^t a_t^b\left(\frac{da_t}{a_t}\right),$$

$$\delta U_t = u\bar{a}^b\Sigma_t\left(\frac{1}{1+r}\right)^t\left(\frac{\delta a_t}{\bar{a} + \delta a_t}\right).$$

When $\sigma_2^* = 0$ and f_1 is constrained to zero, $\delta a_0 = \delta a_2 = 0$, and $\delta a_1 = -(1/\gamma)C_1^s$, giving

81

foreign demand is seen to be permanent ($\sigma_2^* = 1$), then $f_1 = 0$. There is no financing. In this simple case, moreover, outcomes are the same with reserve use and with reserve-credit use. If the disturbance is seen to be temporary, reserves are drawn down by f_1 at $t = 1$ and reconstituted fully at $t = 2$, which is also the pattern of reserve-credit use.

In the next case, the disturbance occurs at $t = 1$ but is anticipated at $t = 0$. With reserve-credit use, $f_0 = 0$ as before, because there is no balance of payments need until $t = 1$, and the optimal outcome is given by attaching asterisks to f_1 and C_1^s in equation 22. With reserve use, however, there are two first-order conditions closely resembling equation 20, and they can be solved for f_0 and f_1^*:

(23)
$$f_0 = -\left(\frac{1}{D}\right)[(2 + i) - (1 - \sigma_2^*)]C_1^s*,$$

$$f_1^* = \left(\frac{1}{D}\right)[(2 + i)(1 - \sigma_2^*) - (1 + i)]C_1^s*,$$

where $D = (2 + i)^2 - (1 + i) = (2 + i) + (1 + i)^2$. If the disturbance is seen to be temporary,

$$f_0 = -\left(\frac{1}{D}\right)(1 + i)C_1^s*,$$

$$f_1^* = \left(\frac{1}{D}\right)C_1^s*,$$

$$f_1^* - f_0 = \left(\frac{1}{D}\right)(2 + i)C_1^s*.$$

Reserves are built up at $t = 0$, run down at $t = 1$, and reconstituted fully at $t = 2$. By building them up at $t = 0$, moreover, the government can run

---

$$\delta U_t^0 = -u\bar{a}^b\left(\frac{1}{1 + r}\right)\left(\frac{C_1^s}{\gamma\bar{a} - C_1^s}\right).$$

When $\sigma_2^* = 0$ but the value of f_1 is given by equation 22, $\delta a_0 = 0$ and $\delta a_1 = \delta a_2 = -[(1 + r)/(2 + r)]C_1^s$, giving

$$\delta U_t^f = -u\bar{a}^b\left(\frac{1}{1 + r}\right)\left[\frac{(2 + r)C_1^s}{(2 + r)\gamma\bar{a} - (1 + r)C_1^s}\right],$$

so that $\delta U_t^f > \delta U_t^0$. These two methods can be used to prove statements made below about welfare changes.

them down farther at $t = 1$ than it could in the previous case; the value of $f_1^* - f_0$ is larger than that implied by equation 22. There is thus more financing with reserve use than with reserve-credit use (and more reserve use when the disturbance is anticipated than when it is not). If the disturbance is seen to be permanent,

$$f_0 = -\left(\frac{1}{D}\right)(2 + i)C_1^s{}^*,$$

$$f_1^* = -\left(\frac{1}{D}\right)C_1^s{}^*,$$

$$f_1^* - f_0 = \left(\frac{1}{D}\right)(1 + i)C_1^s{}^*.$$

Reserves are built up at $t = 0$, run down at $t = 1$, and run down some more at $t = 2$. (They can be run down at $t = 2$ because they are built up by more at $t = 0$ and run down by less at $t = 1$ than they were when the disturbance was temporary.) Note that the result obtained here constitutes an exception to the general rule given in the text that permanent disturbances should not be financed for purposes of maximizing household welfare. The exception arises because the government can reduce real expenditure at $t = 0$, before the disturbance arrives, and thus spread out the permanent reduction imposed by the disturbance at $t = 1$. (By implication, the force of the exception is diluted by extending the planning horizon, and there will be no financing of permanent disturbances, even if anticipated, in an infinite-horizon model.)

In the third case, the disturbance occurs at $t = 0$ and is not anticipated. To minimize the number of comparisons, we look first at a disturbance that is strictly temporary (where $\sigma_1^* = \sigma_2^* = 0$) and one that is strictly permanent (where $\sigma_1^* = \sigma_2^* = 1$). From the first-order condition for optimal reserve-credit use,

(24) $$f_0 = \left(\frac{1}{2 + i}\right)(1 - \sigma_1^*)C_0^s,$$

which is equivalent to equation 22. There is partial financing when the disturbance is strictly temporary and none when it is strictly permanent. From the two first-order conditions for optimal reserve use,

$$f_0 = \left(\frac{1}{D}\right)[(2 + i)(1 - \sigma_1^*) + (\sigma_1^* - \sigma_2^*)]C_0^s,$$

83

(25)

$$f_1^* = \left(\frac{1}{D}\right)[(1 + i)(1 - \sigma_1^*) + (2 + i)(\sigma_1^* - \sigma_2^*)]C_0^s.$$

When the disturbance is strictly temporary,

$$f_0 = \left(\frac{1}{D}\right)(2 + i)C_0^s,$$

$$f_1^* = \left(\frac{1}{D}\right)(1 + i)C_0^s,$$

$$f_1^* - f_0 = -\left(\frac{1}{D}\right)C_0^s.$$

Reserves are run down at $t = 0$, built up at $t = 1$, and built up again at $t = 2$ to reconstitute them fully; and because two periods are available for reconstitution, the amount of financing at $t = 0$ is larger than with reserve-credit use (and larger also than in the first case above, where the disturbance occurred at $t = 1$). Therefore, reserve use raises welfare compared with the level that would obtain with reserve-credit use. This is a simple illustration of the statement in the text that reserve use affords more flexibility. (In this instance, moreover, the advantage of reserve use is increased by extending the planning period; more financing can take place at $t = 0$ because the rebuilding of reserves can be spread over a longer interval. In an infinite-horizon model, $f_0 \to C_0^s$, which is the limiting case of full financing and infinitesimal adjustment.) When the disturbance is strictly permanent, however, $f_0 = f_1 = 0$, and there is no financing.

Before turning to the fourth and final case, involving uncertainty, we look at optimal reserve use when a disturbance lasts for more than one period but is not strictly permanent (where $\sigma_1^* = 1$ but $\sigma_2^* = 0$). From equations 25,

$$f_0 = \left(\frac{1}{D}\right)C_0^s,$$

$$f_1^* = \left(\frac{1}{D}\right)(2 + i)C_0^s,$$

$$f_1^* - f_0 = \left(\frac{1}{D}\right)(1 + i)C_0^s.$$

Reserves are drawn down at $t = 0$ and again at $t = 1$, and all of the rebuilding takes place at $t = 2$. Furthermore, reserve use at $t = 0$ is

84

smaller than when the disturbance was strictly temporary, because there must be more at $t = 1$.

Introducing Uncertainty

Returning to the first case considered above, we introduce uncertainty by supposing that $\sigma_2^* = 1$ with probability α and $\sigma_2^* = 0$ with probability $1 - \alpha$. Setting $\pi_2^* = 0$, as before, and choosing f_1 to maximize expected utility, we obtain the counterpart of equation 20a:

$$(26) \qquad a_1^{b-1} = \left(\frac{1+i}{1+r}\right)[\alpha a_2'^{b-1} + (1 - \alpha)a_2''^{b-1}],$$

where

$$a_1 = \bar{a} + \left(\frac{1}{\gamma}\right)(f_1 - C_1^s),$$

$$a_2' = \bar{a} - \left(\frac{1}{\gamma}\right)[(1 + i)f_1 - C_1^s],$$

$$a_2'' = \bar{a} - \left(\frac{1}{\gamma}\right)(1 + i)f_1.$$

Unfortunately, it is not possible to solve this equation for the optimal value of f_1, although it is possible to show that $0 < f_1 < [1/(2 + i)]C_1^s$ when $0 < \alpha < 1$, which says that f_1 is no larger than the values given by equation 22 for the cases where it is known with certainty that $\sigma_2^* = 1$ and $\sigma_2^* = 0$.

A simple solution can be obtained, however, when households (and the government) are nearly risk neutral and may be deemed to maximize the utility of expected income rather than expected utility. Under this assumption, the terms $E_t a_t^b$ in equation 4a are replaced by the terms $(E_t a_t)^b$, and equation 26 gives way to

$$(26a) \qquad a_1^{b-1} = \left(\frac{1+i}{1+r}\right)[\alpha a_2' + (1 - \alpha)a_2'']^{b-1},$$

so $a_1 = \alpha a_2' + (1 - \alpha)a_2''$, and $f_1 = [1/(2 + i)](1 - \alpha)C_1^s$. There can be no difference between reserve use and reserve-credit use, but there is less financing than when it was known that $\sigma_2^* = 0$ and more than when it was known that $\sigma_2^* = 1$.

The importance of the flexibility conferred by reserve use can be illustrated by risk-neutral behavior in the third case considered above. Suppose that $\sigma_1^* = 1$ with probability α and $\sigma_1^* = 0$ with probability $1 - \alpha$, but $\sigma_2^* = 0$ with certainty. The authorities know that the disturbance will not be strictly permanent but do not know whether it will be strictly temporary or will last for more than one period. With reserve-credit use,

$$f_0 = \left(\frac{1}{2+i}\right)(1 - \alpha)C_0^s,$$

as in the previous example. There will be less financing than when it was known that the disturbance would be strictly temporary but more than when it was known that the disturbance would last for one period. With reserve use, however, the problem is more complicated, because the authorities can take a decision regarding f_1 after the resolution of uncertainty.

Suppose that the authorities draw down reserves by some amount f_0 at $t = 0$. If the disturbance continues at $t = 1$ (that is, $\sigma_1 = 1$), then

$$a_1' = \bar{a} + \left(\frac{1}{\gamma}\right)[f_1' - (1 + i)f_0 - C_0^s],$$

$$a_2'^* = \bar{a} - \left(\frac{1}{\gamma}\right)(1 + i)f_1'.$$

Maximizing U_t at $t = 1$, the authorities will choose

$$f_1' = \left(\frac{1}{2+i}\right)[(1 + i)f_0 + C_0^s],$$

so that

$$a_1' = a_2'^* = \bar{a} - \left(\frac{1}{\gamma}\right)\left(\frac{1+i}{2+i}\right)[(1 + i)f_0 + C_0^s].$$

If the disturbance does not continue at $t = 1$ (that is, $\sigma_1 = 0$), then

$$a_1'' = \bar{a} + \left(\frac{1}{\gamma}\right)[f_1'' - (1 + i)f_0],$$

$$a_2''^* = \bar{a} - \left(\frac{1}{\gamma}\right)(1 + i)f_1''.$$

Maximizing U_t at $t = 1$, the authorities will choose $f''_1 = [(1 + i)/(2 + i)]f_0$, so that

$$a''_1 = a''_2{}^* = \bar{a} - \left(\frac{1}{\gamma}\right)\left(\frac{1 + i}{2 + i}\right)(1 + i)f_0.$$

Using these state-contingent solutions, we obtain the expected values for a_1^* and a_2^* viewed from $t = 0$ (the time at which the authorities must choose f_0):

$$a_1^* = a_2^* = \bar{a} - \left(\frac{1}{\gamma}\right)\left(\frac{1 + i}{2 + i}\right)[(1 + i)f_0 + \alpha C_0^\delta].$$

Proceeding in the usual way, we obtain

$$f_0 = \left(\frac{1}{D}\right)[(2 + i) - \alpha(1 + i)]C_0^\delta,$$

which is subject to the same interpretation as the value obtained for optimal reserve-credit use. But the argument can be carried farther. With reserve-credit use, uncertainty reduces optimal f_0 to $(1 - \alpha)$ of its value when the disturbance is known to be strictly temporary. With reserve use, uncertainty reduces it to $\{1 - [(1 + i)/(2 + i)]\alpha\}$ of its value when the disturbance is known to be strictly temporary. The reduction in f_0 is smaller because the authorities are not bound by fixed-term repayment.

Stabilizing Employment

In all of the cases considered above, the government's only objective was to maximize household welfare. Whenever it engaged in optimal financing, however, it reduced the amount of transitional unemployment resulting from wage rigidity. From equations 10a and 15,

(10b) $\qquad \delta L_k = -\theta(1 - \lambda)[Q_k^\xi + C_k^\xi - (1 - \gamma)\delta a_k].$

There is, of course, no balance of payments financing when the disturbance is an output shock, $(Q_k^\xi > 0)$, or when it is a strictly permanent reduction in foreign demand ($C_k^\xi > 0$ and $\sigma_j^* = 1$ for all j).[98] In other cases,

98. These statements hold only when $\pi_j^* = 0$; see note 95 above.

however, optimal financing offsets part of the reduction in a_k imposed by the disturbance, shrinking the amount of unemployment. When $k = 1$, for example, and the disturbance is unanticipated, $f_1 = [1/(2 + i)]C_1^s$ with both forms of financing, reserve use and reserve-credit use, and the reduction in a_1 falls from $-C_1^s$ to $-[(1 + i)/(2 + i)]C_1^s$.

But a government may want to eliminate transitional unemployment, not merely reduce it, which means that it must choose the value of f_k that satisfies

(27)
$$\delta a_k = \left(\frac{1}{1 - \gamma}\right)(Q_k^s + C_k^s).$$

When $k = 1$, equation 27 fixes f_1 and thus the whole pattern of financing. When $k = 0$, however, equation 27 fixes f_0, and the government can still choose the value of f_1^* that minimizes the welfare cost of stabilizing employment. We look at four examples.

(1) An output shock, $Q_0^s > 0$, whose duration does not matter, because it does not affect a_t directly. In this case, equations 19a and 27 say that $\delta a_0 = (1/\gamma)f_0$, so $f_0 = [\gamma/(1 - \gamma)]Q_0^s$, and $\delta a_1 = f_1^* - (1 + i)[\gamma/(1 - \gamma)]Q_0^s$. When f_1^* is optimized, however, $\delta a_1^* = \delta a_2^*$, as usual, and $\delta a_2^* = -(1 + i)f_1^*$ in this instance, so

$$f_1^* = \left(\frac{1 + i}{2 + i}\right)\left(\frac{\gamma}{1 - \gamma}\right)Q_0^s,$$

$$f_1^* - f_0 = -\left(\frac{1}{2 + i}\right)\left(\frac{\gamma}{1 - \gamma}\right)Q_0^s.$$

Reserves are run down at $t = 0$ to finance the requisite increase in real expenditure. They are rebuilt at $t = 1$ and again at $t = 2$.

(2) A reduction in foreign demand, $C_0^s > 0$, seen to be strictly temporary. In this case, equations 19a and 27 say that $\delta a_0 = (1/\gamma)(f_0 - C_0^s)$, so $f_0 = [1/(1 - \gamma)]C_0^s$, and $\delta a_1^* = f_1^* - (1 + i)[1/(1 - \gamma)]C_0^s$. But $\delta a_2^* = -(1 + i)f_1^*$, as before, so

$$f_1^* = \left(\frac{1 + i}{2 + i}\right)\left(\frac{1}{1 - \gamma}\right)C_0^s,$$

$$f_1^* - f_0 = -\left(\frac{1}{2 + i}\right)\left(\frac{1}{1 - \gamma}\right)C_0^s.$$

88

The pattern of reserve use is the same as in case 1, though each change is bigger by $(1/\gamma)$, and it differs only in detail from the pattern obtained when welfare was maximized without regard to employment effects.[99]

(3) A reduction in foreign demand, $C_0^s > 0$, seen to be permanent. Again, $f_0 = [1/(1 - \gamma)]C_0^s$, but $\delta a_1^* = f_1^* - (1 + i)[1/(1 - \gamma)]C_0^s - C_0^s$, and $\delta a_2^* = -(1 + i)f_1^* - C_0^s$. Nevertheless, the pattern of reserve use is the same as before (because δa_1^* and δa_2^* differ uniformly from their previous values). As in case 1, however, the pattern differs sharply from the one obtained when employment effects were ignored and there was no financing whatsoever.

(4) A reduction in foreign demand, $C_0^s > 0$, seen to last two periods. Again, $f_0 = [1/(1 - \gamma)]C_0^s$, but $\delta a_1^* = f_1^* - (1 + i)[1/(1 - \gamma)]C_0^s - C_0^s$, while $\delta a_2^* = -(1 + i)f_1^*$. Therefore,

$$f_1^* = \left(\frac{1}{2 + i}\right)[(1 + i) + (1 - \gamma)]\left(\frac{1}{1 - \gamma}\right)C_0^s,$$

$$f_1^* - f_0 = -\left(\frac{1}{2 + i}\right)\left(\frac{\gamma}{1 - \gamma}\right)C_0^s.$$

The pattern of reserve use is similar to those in cases 2 and 3, but reserves are built up by less at $t = 1$ and by more at $t = 2$. The pattern is different from the one obtained when employment effects were ignored (as reserves were run down at $t = 1$ but are built up here).

99. In that earlier case, $f_0 = (1/D)(2 + i)C_0^s$, smaller than the value obtained here, and the values of f_1^* and $f_1^* - f_0^*$ were likewise smaller.